The Road to Redemption

Overcoming life's detours, obstacles and challenges

New Conversation
~~for~~ WOOSAH!

LUCINDA CROSS

10/12

The Road To Redemption
Overcoming Life's Detours, Obstacles and Challenges

ISBN 9780615566061

Published by Lucinda Cross

New York, NY

Email: lucinda@lucindacross.com
Website: www.lucindacross.com

Cover Design by Rebekah Jenkins of Innovative Design Style

Edited by Joy Farrington of Lit Diva, Inc

Book Layout by Youdeline A. Holt of Edifying Publishers
Printed in the United States of America

The Road to Redemption:

OVERCOMING LIFE'S DETOURS, OBSTACLES AND CHALLENGES

How to use this book: If you decide to dive in and out of this book expecting a miracle, you have just picked up the wrong book. If you decide to act occasionally on the suggested strategies, you will undoubtedly receive some benefit but it is highly unlikely that you will experience a transformation. In my experience, mindsturbation is the major difference that separates those who receive remarkable results and experience a major transformation from those who enjoy spurts of success. Mindsturbation is a combination of motivation and temporary mental stimulation. People looking for a temporary feel-good will find innumerable ways not to do the recommended success strategies.

The Road To Redemption is more than just another shelf item that you can read to get a quick fix, steps to, or how to advice book. This is a story of REDEMPTION. This is a process. Activation is required; the change does not happen overnight and requires you to focus fully on your destination in life. Many of us have become so self-sabotaged that we are just tired of being tired. Many of us have given up too soon, right before our breakthrough in life. Many of us have lost our hope and faith and have pulled back from being spiritually connected. Many of us have been motivated and empowered to experience only confusion, loneliness, self-doubt, and feelings of unworthiness. This has opened the door to saying yes, when we wanted to say no, to become unproductive because we allowed distractions and competition to hinder the completion of our process.

The Road to Redemption is designed to teach us to check our character, spiritual beliefs, mindset, relationships, and skill sets. Too often, our intellectual assets are underdeveloped, underutilized, or underperformed. *The Road to Redemption* will help you reach, stretch, grow, and propel into becoming the greatest and best YOU.

You must read this book with a willing and able mindset that commits itself to the following:

- I am open to change my life dramatically despite the odds.
- I will read this book carefully, using my highlighter to mark statements that stand out and commentaries that capture my attention.
- I will begin to keep a journal.
- I will invest my time into reading this book from cover to cover.
- I will share this process with family, friends, and colleagues. Anybody within one foot of me will hear about the process that takes place within.
- I recognize that this book is merely a starting point. I am willing to launch into a path of awareness and growth that will take time to develop and I am excited about the process.
- I recognize that there is a need to release disempowering belief systems and bad habits to live a life of meaning, purpose, and fulfillment.
- I will read and reflect on the points that ignite me, write my insights in a journal then I will immediately act on what I have read.

Remember: Your journal will reveal your progress, so keep it with you always.

To God Be the Glory

Table of Contents

Acknowledgments

First God the Father for the testimony, my Bishop R.J Stockton III, for anointing my hands every time I had writers block, my mom and dad for loving me and believing in me. My husband for always pushing me to go higher and always holding me accountable. To my babies Khallid, Khayla, Zahir and Cam for keeping me on my toes and reminding me that you want expensive things. All my family and friends and my lovely spiritual mothers Minister Kim, Minister Angela M. Williams and First Lady Tiffany Stockton for pushing me to be transparent according to God's timing, for keeping me in prayer, covering me in prayer and loving me with the love of God. A special shout out to my DMV crew and my Social Media family. Special thanks to Kadena Tate for the push I needed every time I needed it. Thanks to Youdeline Holt for holding my hand through the complete book process, you are my midwife.

Welcome

We've all been there at that make it or break it moment in our lives. That moment where it seems as if time stops and the world is spinning, but you are not moving. You may even feel like you are stuck at a green light and can't move forward or Pass Go to collect $200. You have a decision to make. You have an obstacle in front of you that you did not expect or did not suspect it to be.

Maybe you haven't attained the success you feel your hard work should have brought you by now or maybe you feel you have the talent to be all that you can be, be the expert in your field, but you just can't seem to put that talent or those skills into position to be useful when it really counts.

Maybe just maybe you feel your potential or this gift you have just isn't being tapped and you have no clue what's missing or what's holding you back.

You are keen on not wasting any more time wallowing and wandering in the self- pity party. You're not interested in looking back into your childhood; you simply want to move forward. You don't want to be sabotaged by self-doubt any longer. You don't want to be paralyzed by pressure or fear. You want to accomplish a goal or that 2nd chance to complete your unfinished life work, that will tap your full potential and you want courage and determination to go after that vision, no matter how unrealistic, out of your mind it may seem to others, no matter how much heat you have to endure, no matter how many setbacks you have to fight to overcome.

You are in full pursuit of success and happiness.

We are all fighting this fight on a daily basis.

This book can help. This book will help. It encapsulates a program that transformed people in all walks of life. I have been on a mission to bring out peoples best, no matter what they did in the past or what they do for a living.

I learned that my audience lacked self-confidence, feared the unknown, terrified of failure, couldn't focus or concentrate, they were fear paralyzed and mistakes from their past hindered them or haunted them, just like they did to me every time I wanted to move forward.

This book is designed to help each reader to overcome their obstacles in 7 major areas.

• Clarity

• Determination

• Action

• Intention

• Mindset

• Courage

• Discovery

The information provided in this book is about creating the future, not trying to erase the past; about uplifting, inspiring and empowering you to make lasting changes, not excuses for what has already happened.

Whatever success you envision, whatever you are called to do, whatever goal you set for yourself, I want you to see it as your choice and chance to make a difference in your life and the lives of others. My job in these pages is to empower you to make the decisions you deem necessary to achieve your goals and live your best life, the best way you know how.

To be empowered and activated, one must also be inspired. To that end I've included my story of change on my personal Road To Redemption.

No journey can begin, no route can be plotted, and no mission can be accomplished without you taking the first step to make a decision.

What are your intentions in reading this book?

What do you hope to gain?

Where do you stand in your life right now?

You can clearly add your own journey and road map on your Road To Redemption. You can do this; you can change your portion of the people in the world. I will support you to get you through it. I will talk you through it, but you must be ready to meet me at the start line, right where the yellow brick road begins.

I know that whoever you are, whatever you have achieved so far in your life, whatever challenges and obstacles you may be currently experiencing, **it is your hunger for results, real-time information, or something you need to hear again** that will help unlock you. As a traveler on this journey in this process called life, I congratulate you on your commitment and investment to make a shift.

The Road to Redemption depends on my process and my observation of those who have pushed through the doors, waited for someone to open the doors, and those who just sat by the doors, waiting for a window of opportunity when it was the door that needed to be opened, not the window.

This book is similar to a guidebook and its design fits easily into your busy lifestyle by taking these bite size pieces of food for the soul to digest each day in a matter of minutes. You will go from understanding the power of making decisions to valuing your relationships, your health, your emotions, and your finances.

Thank you for the gift of allowing me to share these commentaries with you. I know that you will find something in this book, even in a single sentence, a compelling thought, a powerful idea, that will move you in a special way to act in your life. I look forward to meeting you in person one day soon.

Give yourself the gift of undivided attention and enjoy the journey.

Lucinda Cross

Introduction:
The Transformation Process

- What if the caterpillar never emerged out of the cocoon?
- What if she dreaded to let go of her old habits and dreaded to embrace her new abilities?
- What if she worried about the old shell that she left and wanted to carry it with her when she set out to fly?
- What if she never allowed the old body to die (in order) for her to soar in her true potential and power?
- What if she sat there and wondered about the "how" this happened to her as opposed to the "what" she can now do such as, fly freely, travel, be among other fliers?

Many people use the butterfly as an example of transformation. I want you to look at the process that the caterpillar goes through to become that beautiful, colorful, and freedom flier that it is. You too can become that butterfly, once you realize that the cocoon is a place for development and preparation. If you are in the cocoon phase, then allow the soul to search the insides to see what needs to die and what needs to mature to fly freely when its time.

The transformation process is not easy and it is a series of restoration, renewing, releasing, refining, and repurposing us from the inside out. Check out and ponder a process that is not easy, and think about where you are in your life right now in the transformation process.

Inside the cocoon, the caterpillar changes into a pupa. In a process called histolysis, the caterpillar digests itself from the inside out, causing its body to die. During this partial death, the caterpillar salvages some of its old tissues to form new. These remnants of cells are called the histoblasts and are used to generate a new body. Using its digestive juices, the caterpillar turns his old larval body into food, which he uses to rebuild its new body. If you are in the process to go deeper, the process of going inside to weed out the unwanted or unnecessary things, embrace it. Know that you are going to come out as a beautiful butterfly.

Chapter 1:
Everybody Has A Past

- How do you move past the past when the world is telling you, you are not enough?
- How do you move on and keep your eyes on the prize when all odds are against you?
- How do you activate when life is more than uncomfortable and the challenges and obstacles are real, and they just keep coming?

In my observation of success, I concluded that success is defined on your own terms. To me, success comes in the form of loving relationships, time with my family, health, and a lifestyle full of opportunities. Success means simplistic things that life gives us free, such as freedom to dream, freedom to believe, and freedom to love. You know those things that we take for granted then cry about when they are removed from us.

This was not always my belief. I thought I was failing in life when my world turned upside down. The dreams that my parents had for me had taken a turn in a nightmare they would have never thought or imagined.

Let me share a story that has never been told. This is a story of my past, my mistakes, and my *Road to Redemption*. We all have a road we have traveled but many of us will never have the opportunity to tell it, because we are living up to society's dogmas and endorsements. Everyone reading this book is now getting the other side of my determination and motivation. I talk about the story of being a Corporate Mom Drop Out with three children, a wife that manages it all, business adviser that continues to inspire women to move forward with force and a mentor to those who need to activate.

- How did this all come about?
- What is the testimony that keeps the drive on automatic?

Here is my story as a troubled teen, who later grew up as a responsible adult.

I remember the day clearly when I was arrested. More than thirty cops, guns drawn, helicopter in the air, surrounding my complete apartment complex and swarmed around my house as if I were on the *America's Most Wanted*. I was nineteen and never had been arrested for anything. I came from a good family who had good jobs.

My mother was a college graduate, and the man I call dad from age two and whom I consider my father was an Army veteran who gave me more love than any father could give his little girl.

I was the oldest of three siblings and that meant that Lucinda had to be sister, mom, the firstborn, but the last to receive. I had a wonderful childhood and watched how my mother tried her best to "make do". This inspired me to try to make life better for both my family and myself, but the road I decided to take was one often traveled but revealed less often. I am revealing it to free myself, and those walking around with monkeys on their back and mask on their face.

In 1996, I traded in four years of college for four and half years in Federal prison and five on probation. Yes, you read that last line correctly. I was in college just as any other guided and well-informed teenager who just graduated out of High school. I had dreams of being a nurse or a lawyer. I had dreams of providing for my family and making my parents proud. I had dreams of getting out of the projects and moving into a big house with a pool. I had dreams of joining a Sorority and supporting my community. I had dreams of becoming that good Christian that my pastor always talked about during Sunday mornings just before the choir sings another song. Just as most high school girls with the world in her hands, I had dreams of traveling the world, learning new languages, even modeling and being on Television. Dreams of becoming the best me I could be.

Well, five months into my studies I was approached with an offer that was difficult to refuse. An opportunity of a lifetime, I thought, I was offered a quick fix and it meant I could speed up my process and provide for my family. Heck, here was an opportunity to make in a matter of months what my parents made in one year. I had traveled to Thailand, Japan, Singapore, Amsterdam, Cambodia, China, Vietnam, Mexico, and some local states such as Texas, Michigan, and so on. I was getting $15,000 each trip.

I was playing the role of a model, I was traveling the world, I was learning new languages, and I was "living a fantasy, not my dream." I was putting money in the community, buying clothes, sneakers, motorcycles -- whatever they wanted, I provided. I did not have to worry about sitting in the college cafeteria at Iona College watching the fortunate children eat and network while I had to find a way to make it home on an empty stomach. How do you explain to a first-year student in college who is hungry and barely making it with her part-time job that $15,000 is not a good idea? It was fast, it was believable, and for a child with a dream and unsure how to make it work, it was all I had and something I felt would give me Hope.

Later I quickly discovered this was not my dream instead a deceptive reality. I traveled for six months as a transporter. My job was to move when the mule moved or so I thought, only to discover I was a mule, a transporter, a carrier. As I travelled from place to place, walked around, took pictures, shopped and acted as if I were a model, I would wait for the bat phone to ring to catch the the net thing smoking out of the country to my next location.

- Was I scared? Nope
- Was I afraid? Nope

I was determined and focused to get to the finish line to get my money. I was hungry, I was bold, and I was fearless. I used all the right characteristics for the wrong thing. I know you have been there before, where you find yourself being strong at the wrong time, being assertive and upset at the wrong people, making the wrong decision out of feelings, lack of vision or simple people pleasing. Well this was one of those courage and determination for the wrong pursuit type of situations.

The saying that goes "patience is a virtue" is important when it is time to endure.

Write this in big bold red letters "Patience is a virtue" inside your journal, here is why.

Had I stayed in school, waited patiently, my breakthrough would have come. Had I waited for opportunities to pursue my dream instead of moving in haste to make a decision that changed my life forever, my time would have come.

Do not let anyone alter your vision, change your dream, or dilute your future. I do not care what it looks like now. You hold that vision; you pursue that dream, and know that you have to be patient.

Losing my patience led me down a six-month international journey, until there was a knock on my door that I would never forget. The banging was hard and thunderous, enough to shake your soul. As my baby brothers remained asleep waiting for me to wake them for school, my mom and dad off to work, my mom's house was turned upside down and inside out as I am being questioned about my lavish trips and countless western unions. That was 1996, the beginning of the next five years "living life outside of my comfort zone." My brothers never made it to school that morning and my mother was terrified as I tried to calm her as she seen her "college daughter, model and baby girl with dreams" get cuffed and escorted out of her house to never return to that house the same little girl again.

The environment was a shock, to say the least. A young college girl had to grow up fast and I mean real fast. I did much soul searching and much dreaming. An old prison mother gave me a saying that helped me throughout the rest of my experience, "Do your time, don't let your time do you." This was all I could think about after countless hours of crying, wondering, and hoping to get home.

Have you ever been removed out of your comfort zone and had to adjust to a new environment or a new location? Maybe you have gone through a divorce that forced you out of your comfy home, or losing your house forcing you to downsize, or becoming unemployed forcing you to go to social service or unemployment. Being positioned away from your comfort zone, away from the day-to-day operations that you can control. This was the time. When it is out of your control you have to "do the time and not let the time do you". This means is that you have to change your reaction to unfortunate circumstances as opposed letting your unfortunate circumstances change who you are and your character.

In this situation where I was isolated from the world, I was still determined to dream again, to try again, and to live again and this meant that I had to remove my mindset from the current situation and find freedom behind bars with no mommy to cry to, no daddy to lean on, no Nana to pray with. I had to rely on my memory, thus begin to take everything that I remembered and use it to keep me whole in a place of brokenness, barrenness, and barred both literally and figuratively.

Living behind bars has taught me the human spirit, the patience, diligence, determination of people on a mission to "do the time rather than let the time do them. How are you doing your time now? How do you dream again, believe again, and try again, when the world is telling you, you are not enough? How do you push forward when the odds are against you? How do you activate when life is more than uncomfortable, the challenges and obstacles are real, and they keep coming?

Many people in the community are mentally locked down. I have run across more people behind bars who are more mentally free than the man you see walking down the street.

Remember everybody has a past. It is important to learn how to reinvent yourself so your past mistakes are your now miracles and a key to unlock someone else's dream. Break down those mental and emotional bars and be free. The power that a situation and I mean any situation has over us is not in the situation or circumstance, but in what we think of the situation. We don't change the situation or the challenge that is ahead, but we can change the way we see it. And when you do decide to remove those bars from your mind, we are no longer a victim; we are asserting our control over our emotions and moving from victim to problem solver, to freedom fighter, to a power house.

Can you see how removing the emotional and mental bars change the dynamic of your situation? I know for sure it changed mine. Most of our worst experiences come from playing mind games with ourselves. "Why can't I get it right?" "Why is this always happening to me?", "How did I get here again and again and again?" This is the blame game. Remember you have the power to revoke any negative or self serving thoughts or views at any moment, but it is completely up to you to make the choice that enough is enough.

I need you to understand that there is something phenomenal going on in you. During my reinvention, there was something phenomenal going on within me. It does not feel comfortable during the process and sometimes life gives us each a different kind of reinvention and physical position for the real you, the real Lucinda Cross to stand in her power and speak her truth.

During your reinvention, you will begin to feel the following:

- Somewhat uncomfortable...
- Pushed and pulled to do something else...
- Cry because things are not working out...

- Impatient with the level of success you have now and ready to up level…
- Feel as if what you want to do is not what you are supposed to do…
- Over excited as if something is about to happen…
- Sad at times as if something is fading or dying inside…

Well the feelings that you have been experiencing are symptoms of what I observed as the process of "REINVENTION".

Reinvention goes hand in hand with patience. Patience is the act of waiting and reinvention is the process of creating something new. It is all part of the process. Waiting for your time and your turn. Waiting is one of the hardest things for us human beings to do; we want everything quick, fast, and in a hurry. Sometimes life forces us to slow and if we really force the hand of time, it may force us to stop altogether.

That was the case with me. You never know if the road you are traveling is heading in the right direction unless you stop to look at the road map, look at the compass to make sure you are not making u-turns around the same obstacles and stumbling blocks. I was impatient and wanted things my way, quick fast and in a hurry. I wanted to reinvent myself instead of allowing life to take its course. Instead of following the road often traveled, I wanted to find a way to get out of poverty, lack, disappointment, and suffering by my own strength.

Sidebar: that will never work; always let go and let God. I repeat, do not force yourself into a bottomless valley, be patient, and wait for instruction. Change will come, and with change are your reinvention and your breakthrough.

Reinventing yourself may come as a brand change, a new direction in your business or life, a shift in your relationships, beliefs, and inner circle. It will not be easy or comfortable but heed the WARNING; you might have to experience some withdrawal symptoms before you fully get there. Letting go is not easy, and being patient is not easy. What I am saying is that it is time to adjust toward the shifting within, so begin to change by saying:

- I am free from unhealthy relationships and people, even call some names out
- I am moving in divine timing
- I embrace change
- I give myself permission to be unapologetically me
- I am free
- I am me
- I am accepted
- I am reinvented

When something phenomenal is going on in you, you have no choice but to strip out the weeds surrounding you and begin to help the real you breathe and become visible.

My reinvention came as a complete stripping of the outer layer to get to the core that is the Lucinda Cross you know today. No fancy hairdo, no Mani or Pedi, no fancy clothes and expensive shoes, no sushi and expensive dinners and lunches, no money to flash, no name- just an eight-digit number and an orange suit or sweats. Now, I was forced to deal with who Lucinda Cross really was. I had no choice but to spend some time with myself and to see exactly what I comprised, without the worldly attachments and luxuries. The peeling begins…

Can you do that? Can you spend time with yourself to really identify who you are? Many people are walking zombies; they are breathing and walking but have no clue of what they comprise.

I know what these zombies look like because I was one of those zombies or rather a robot. As a zombie if you told me what to do or what you wanted, I felt compelled to do it or make it happen. I was a people pleaser and not a God pleaser. Not knowing who you are and what you offer is disempowering, allow this to be the first step you take. Know who you are and whose you are.

The ability to reinvent yourself is one of the key tools you need to stay ahead of the game we call life. To endure your *Road to Redemption*. Your reinvention process begins with letting go of the crippling dis-EASE to please. This reinvention process helps you stand tall in business and in life. You start to devise new ideas, new ways to look at life and those in your life. You begin to cultivate productive habits and constructive relationships despite where you are.

It makes no sense to operate life with nonproductive habits.

If your business or relationships are broken or unsustainable and you have given it your all, do not wait too long before you decide to change and begin the reinvention process. That is why I say something phenomenal is going on.

It has to do with change, growth, and evolution. It has to do with women, and moms, men and fathers. It has something to do with a higher force, God. When we allow ourselves to go through the reinvention process, there are changes taking place in the hearts and minds of us that are going to rock this world literally.

What role are you playing in your life and others? Do you need to reinvent yourself? Remember that once you decide to begin the reinvention process all the people and things around you will begin to align itself with your purpose, so be clear on what you want and be willing to embrace the change that is about to happen. Do not fight it embrace it.

Chapter 2: Work it!

Everything you do and do not do is paid for with a price. Inner strength is something we must all build daily such as a physical workout. I had to learn this the hard way. Being transferred from Metropolitan Correction Center in NY to MCC Chicago and placed in solitary confinement for nine months was nothing like they show on television. This was the real deal, cold, the aroma of death and the atmosphere reeked the sour scent of fear and frustration. Controlled lightning, controlled air, controlled shower times, controlled recreation, controlled minds is what was waiting for me. This roadblock felt like a ton of bricks on my heart. I was told that until the judge approves my release I could join general population; my lawyer told me that I had twenty-eight codefendants in general population and they wanted to make sure that we could all just get along.

My response to this was... What? Twenty-eight who? Problems? Solitary confinement? Are you kidding me? Where is my mommy? I do not want to go through this anymore. God why me? I am sorry...I just wanted to.... I did not mean to...twenty-three-hour lockdown.

Here is a situation where any human being with warm blood in their body would have freaked out. I know I did but when you look at how in some situations it appears as if everything is stripped away and God is commanding your full attention. Well this was the case for me and I guess he had to go to the extreme in order to get me to wake up. The beauty of the solitary confinement moment in those life situations is that we are not alone. No one walks this valley of the shadow of death alone. One of the most comforting and consoling blessings given to us is found in the Bible: "Fear not, for I am with you always." Those words are powerful and should be remembered when you going through your process. This is the strength you need and the assurance to face any obstacle or challenge.

Twenty-three-hour lockdown, did you read that right. Twenty-three-hour lockdown, no sunlight, no workout except a hard steel bike in a Plexiglass room. TOTAL ISOLATION IS AN UNDERSTATEMENT! The only female down there was my codefendant and god-sister who I convinced to "get money" with me and jammed her all up at eighteen. Surrounded by murderers, gang leaders, crooked cops; you name it we were down in the trenches together, some never to see the day of light again. At this point, you can imagine my sleepless nights, tuning out the sounds of grown men crying for freedom, crying because of the deep depression of being caged in like an animal.

They were mentally free and did not know it nor did they care. I started to take this time of solitude as a time to get my beliefs in order, I knew that the only way out of this twenty-three-hour lockdown was to focus on God, focus on getting strength from a source and power much higher and superior to myself. Guess what? It worked. I thank God for the endurance when I wanted to go completely insane, the strength when I felt as if I were going to snap, and the encouragement when I knew for sure that I could not take anymore.

- How many of us need to get ourselves into a place of solitude to discover how strong you are and how powerful you are, to discover whom you are and why you are here?

- When is the last time you pulled yourself away from the business to really see what is ahead, to really see that you can make it and will make it if you just focus on the one thing that is stronger, wiser, and more powerful than you are?

• Where do you get your strength?

Many of us forget to work it, work with what we have to build our inner strength. When you work it, you will realize you have more than enough to make it through whatever you are going through or growing through without losing your mind.

During that time, I learned that my current position had nothing to do with my future position. I knew that this too will pass and that is the only thing that kept me sane. I examined my surroundings and examining my surroundings, I noticed how much pressure the world puts on us. Forcing us to conform to the point where many of us crack in the face of adversity instead of strategizing a way out or in. This is where your inner strength is required to be spiritually, physically, and mentally equipped for the rest of the journey.

• How many times have you allowed your living arrangement to alter your capabilities?
• How many times have you allowed a setback to stop you from putting your best foot forward?
• How many times have you allowed others to control your mind? Instead of saying a strong No you gave a weak Yes and regretted it later?

- How often in the past or maybe even now have you allowed your vision and dreams to fade because you were too busy telling God your problems instead of telling your problems about your God?

It does not matter what you are going through or what the situation may look like, you can only limit yourself. The bars that I had to face everyday did not keep me from believing in me. I learned how to use what I had, and that was the power to believe again, dream again and know that I can get one more try at life again. I encourage you today to do it all again. Give it one more try. Your life, your family and your true friends deserve to see you go at it again, working it, working with what you have to live an amazing life, despite what it looks like now, or what it looked like then.

To experience a breakthrough there are crucial and time sensitive steps you must take: the first step requires you to get a larger vision and stop thinking in terms of the small cell you have guarded, trapped and have locked yourself in. You must go through a continuing shift in your psyche that focuses on your value. Do not worry about the background singers, the inner conversations that tell you that you cannot, you are too short, too tall, too light, too dark, too educated, too uneducated, too this and too that. LEARN TO BLOCK IT ALL OUT, it ONLY matters if you acknowledge and feed into it.

GOD DID IT

After nine-long months of dealing with a variety of personalities, mood swings, mentally unstable people, and unhealthy characters, I finally went upstairs to meet my codefendants, who were my sisters for the next twenty-four months before the pronouncement of my sentence -- one of the most profound experiences in my life so far. Having no choice but to look at who Lucinda is, what Lucinda wants out of life, why Lucinda did what she did, and when Lucinda gets out how she is going to seize every opportunity and breathe life into all of those I encountered who were yearning for an Exodus experience.

- Just think about it, how are you going to activate and move forward when you have been plucked, set apart, and now exposed?
- How are you going to activate all that you have encountered in your quiet time and now faced with another challenge?
- How are you going to push when you are knocked down and life tries to knock you off course?
- How can you remove your mental stigmas and barriers to redeem yourself and free others?
- When you look at your life and you look at your business/career how are you showing up in the world? What are you wearing, or rather, what wears you? Are you presenting yourself with a symbol of worthiness? What boots are you wearing and are they strapped up ready for the next milestone ahead?

It is so important to walk your walk with resilience, and talk with power wrapped in conviction, saying what you mean and meaning what you say. This may sound cliché, but guess what it only works when you work it. Using your last learning lesson to unlock and overcoming the "what's next".

I had the same routine every day, shower, eat, sleep, clean, eat again, write, pray, sleep, TV and occasional game of spades. The highlight of my day was taking time to watch Creflo Dollar, have an imaginary mentoring session with Toni Robbins through his books, meditate on visits from angels and envision myself being free. I started to keep hold of the vision boarding exercise, I decided to write a business plan and draw out a well-written plan to execute when I came home. My coaching and consulting started here, consoling women who were stressed, depressed, used, forgotten, misled, hoodwinked and bamboozled, detoxing, healing, angry, hurting, defensive, offensive, missing their families and children, friends and lifestyle, they all had a story to tell and all shared a deep bond of survival in a place that is designed to break you down, but Lucinda remained Lucinda despite it all, despite my surrounding, I refused to be conformed but transformed. I kept my spirits high; I carried energy with me that I wanted to bring humor, love, and non-judgment in any conversation.

- Can you stay true to yourself when staying true means standing out?

- Can you light up a room by putting your cares to the side to help someone else who is hurting?
- Are you willing to take the time to heal your wounds so you can show others how to heal theirs as well?
- Are you willing to get out of the pity party and shift the atmosphere to uplift and empower those who need encouragement?

After being released, adjusting mentally was difficult for me because I was accustomed to being in a space where everyone operated from authentic self, which in prison is all you have. We did not have time to put on a mask and hide our fears, or put on a mask and fake it till we made it, it was literally do or die, cry, tell the truth or lie, and when you have decisions that need to be made, make sure your Yes is powerful and your No is strong. Stripped from all EGOs we dwell in an organic space doing the time and not letting the time do us, well some of us anyway.

In society, I see how people are getting physically sick everyday by doing something they do not want to do, going to a job they do not like, and staying in unhealthy relationships that tear them down mentally and emotionally just because they feel trapped, obligated and do not know how to release the chains or break free. No matter the prison, you can unlock the chains and become FREE, but it is up to you. No book, no CD, conference, workshop, or coach will do it completely for you. You have to give yourself permission to live without shackles or the stigmas. I have been there and done that and have the T-shirt and mug shot to prove it, no seriously, I do.

You have to start feeling WORTHY. Start to practice saying YES. Yes to your LIFE, yes to your FUTURE and yes to your POTENTIAL. This is when you will see what you are working with, and figure out how to use it to go to the next destination or next chapter in your life.

You can do anything you set your mind to, if and this is a big if, if you are willing to put in the work. I mean some elbow grease. Change is not easy and using your potential gets even harder. It is amazing the opportunities you get and the strength you feel when you take complete responsibility for your choices in life. As you start to make bold, wise and fearless choices you'll start to realize that great potential has always been within you.

Think about what bold choice can you make this year?

What fearless move you can take this month?

How can you exercise your unlimited potential today?

Many of us don't recognize the great potential we all have. When I say potential I am talking about that "thing" that "something" that is there but isn't being used. For some reason many of us think that other people can be successful and powerful in their position because they have that "thing" and we don't. The only difference is that they said YES to their potential and the opportunities that followed and you haven't, we haven't. As long as you walk around thinking that the regular Joe or Jane like us can't do it, we instantly paralyze ourselves and guess what? Confusion, low self esteem and envy come creeping around the corner. The solution is easy. The solution is a simple and courageous YES. Saying YES is the perfect place to start. Begin to eliminate the "I can't" and the "I will try" from your vocabulary. Just do it. Use your unlimited potential.

Repeat after me:

This is my season; I declare this is my season. I give myself permission to be free, I am worthy to be loved, and I am worthy to be wealthy.

In this season, you have to activate your own power, motivate yourself when no one is there to cheer you on, and use what you have to get what you want. I dare you to plug in. What happens to us many times is that we get satisfied and we procrastinate.

Not feeling worthy of your goal will cause you to have distractions. Complaining and never looking for an outcome or solution, just looking at the current situations will cause you to never do anything but sit there boosting everybody, becoming the cheerleader for everybody else. Procrastination causes many of us to take a sabbatical watching others rise to the occasion and being fully present in their lives, while we stay stuck on "what had happened was…" The exciting thing about giving yourself permission is that you open up all that greatness inside you.

You have talents and skills that no one else has and you have your name all over them. What makes me sad is that many of you are not willing to stretch. I had to stretch pass stereotypes, ridicule, and mixed messages of people telling me I messed up my life, and those who never give you space to redeem yourself.

I want you to remember to write it down. I will wait while you get a pencil or pen…"You don't get in life what you want, you get what, and who you are" so put in the work and work it. Despite my position, circumstance, or situation, it did not change my gifts, talents, skills, or abilities. Despite my position, it did not define me or limit me from being worthy. Repeat after me "I am fearfully and wonderfully made" say that three times and take a deep breath.

Ask yourself these questions, but reflect on them before answering them.

- Who do you need to be?
- What do you need to do?
- To have the life you crave to live?

I WANT YOU TO TAKE TWO STEPS TODAY

- The first step is, I want you to decide what you intend to create.
- The second step is to believe you deserve the right to have the best and live the best according to your divine purpose.

Here are more quick questions.

- What brings you joy? (Only you know the answer to this)
- What makes your heart melt? (No not the fondue or the chocolate covered strawberries)
- What do you want to be in business for? (besides sleeping late)
- What does wealth look like to you? (Get a visual; you know I am all about the vision)
- What percentage of you are you willing to give to others? (Without burning yourself out)

When deciding to leave my job there were many reasons for my departure, and my children were 40% of the reason and the other 60% was because I believed in myself. I knew I was not operating in my best, doing my best and becoming the best mom, sister, daughter, or friend I could be.

I was mentally abusing myself by staying at a job that caused me pain that I carried home with me everyday both mentally, emotionally and physically. After my release and living life outside of my comfort zone, I vowed that I, Lucinda Cross was not ONLY going to be unstoppable, but unpredictable...there is no excuses.

The stakes were high with all the bets placed and the gossip committee was in full effect, but it would NOT stop nor hinder me. Determined to live on God's term and not letting folks distract me. I made a firm decision that I would NOT live up, not to the naysayers or the statistic counters that wrote me off long ago. Giving up was not an option and neither was giving in.

Mastering the best me was one of my goals, this is when my *Road to Redemption* began. Living boldly, yearly I declared and proclaimed, "This is my year to elevate".

LOOKING AHEAD, WHILE PRESSING FORWARD

For you to declare this is your year, you MUST to get out of your comfort zone(s), be bold and begin to think "in" the box. When changing the way you think you will need to utilize all the resources around you with a positive and hopeful attitude. The keywords here are *hopeful attitude,* and having said that, you know that whatever you are willing to do, you MUST be Willing to Do Whatever It Takes, DWIT.

Working with what you have and feeling worthy of success will require you to stay hungry, but careful not to eat just anything; you have to understand you are Pregnant with Power. You will have cravings for information, but again be careful what you consume as you are going to be stretched, and you are going to be uncomfortable.

This is a necessary process you have to go through to GROW to who you are destined to be. A change maker, a challenger a visionary…yes that is YOU, so keep pushing it will manifest!

IT IS GOING TO TAKE A YES

When you decide to say Yes -- to your Season, to your Life, to your Destiny, to your Book, to your audio CD, to Yourself, to your Business, to your Education -- that is when the process of conception will take place, and it is not going to be easy. Get ready to PUSH pass your fears and doubts.

One of my first goals I made when I returned home from prison was to graduate from College and start a business. When I made that decision guess what happened, resources showed up, opportunities showed up, my mentor showed up and most of all I could free my mind because I SHOWED UP PREPARED TO GO AND BE ME. Yes, my relationships dwindled during the time I was behind bars; my friendships diminished because of my situation, not based on who I was but where I went, because of my process and my journey.

DECIDE TO MAKE A DECISION

Not everyone is going to understand your vision, path, or value you bring to the table. You have a mission to complete; you have a mandate on your life to fulfill. You have to decide without the voice or influence of others. My family thought I was crazy because I had left my job but they are not supposed to understand my calling.

Out of my adversity lay my freedom, both in being incarcerated and in my life on the outside. Life kept throwing me blow after blow, after blow, nonstop, notwithstanding I do take full responsibility for stepping into the ring that caused me to lose my freedom, but I refused to be counted out, totally knocked out from life and what it had to offer. I had to stand and say, "I'm not going to give up, I have a purpose, and I have a life". I have a reason to believe that things will turn around and things will get better regardless.

Not only do I have a purpose, but also now I know I have a purpose driven life, I am free to fight for its future. I had to remind myself, that my adversity is what makes me a strong businessperson, a strong mother, and a strong woman. I knew that this business idea, this vision of wealth that I had would take more than a good idea and a good character. I had to get real again with myself. I had to remember my calling.

Keep in mind your thoughts become things, so speak greatness over you and the legacy you intend to create. Carefully, I continually remind myself that my vision will take me places I cannot even imagine.

QUESTIONS TO THINK ABOUT:

- Where are you?
- When is the last time you called on the real you?
- When is the last time you told your story and freed yourself?
- When was the last the time you used your authentic voice?

GET BACK UP AGAIN

I had been knocked down, dragged out, shackled up, caged in, and stumbled on, all the while losing something as precious as my freedom. What is it going to take for you to get back up again? To take a stand and get your voice back. What is it going to take for you to realize that the beating life dished out did not break you that you are still standing striving and thriving? What is it going to take for you to remain centered in courage? Ready to drop the pity party bed and have a liberation celebration.

Once upon a time, I allowed others, situations, my past, friends, friendemies, jobs and much more to cause identity theft on me and my dreams by trying to steal my future, my now moments. (I take them all back).

I allowed the past to cloud my future. I gave it permission to do so, therefore, take some time right now, and put the past behind you to live in the land of more than enough, living in abundance knowing that I have been redeemed. In the past, I allowed situations to deter me from using my gifts, talents skills, and abilities for growth.

What doesn't kill you make you stronger. I know you have heard that before. You have a great gift to bring to the world. What happens when we identify that gift or someone points it out for us, we don't sharpen or polish up our gifts. We must do an inner evaluation in order to handle the outer work we need to do. The inner work is your vision, your purpose and your values. This helps you to identify okay what am I here? What do I do next? And who do I do it for? Once you have the answers to at least two of these questions, then you have evidence of the inner work being built. You know how you are, you know whose you are, you know why you are here and you don't need validation from anyone.

People will get nervous, think your acting shady, brand new, weird, or maybe taking this "inner work" too serious but it is necessary and that is why the inner work is so important. The clarity comes from isolation, prayer, fasting, and courage, getting back up again and grabbing a can of fearless fighter on your way out the door. Not having the inner work done will cause you to slow down by people who don't have the courage to do it themselves. They will try to "support" you by telling you to take it easy, slow down, what is your plan B? Getting the inner work done will help you to say boldly, "No thanks" to that kind of "support. You have won your first round of obstacles and challenges when you can face the world and find undiscovered reserves of faith, hope and courage within.

I am here to tell you, it takes more than marketing, sales techniques, twelve-step programs, secrets, and strategies to reach and attain your goals while building loving relationships in conjunction with sustaining business. It takes plenty of energy to do all the above. Any road toward greatness takes plenty of stamina and erraticism. You must be fit mentally to pull away from the very thing, people and habits that want to keep you stuck. The newfound strength that you gain will feel like a tug of war, an ebb and flow of standing tall on self-confidence, then stronger attacks of self-doubt. This will go on until you overcome them; until you can look the fear in the face and say "I am not afraid anymore" I am not afraid of you anymore".

STRETCH YOUR GIFT

Your gift is a work of art. It is meant to be stretched, pulled, used, and restored. Lose your vagueness that you have about yourself, your values, and your life situation. Become available in whatever position or situation you find yourself. This is where solitude comes in handy, I do not recommend a twenty-three-hour lockdown that I had to endure but take some time to get still so you can connect with the authenticity of your gift. The more you stretch your gift the more you gain and align yourself with truth. When we become original, we start to shift into our position and discard the old you while celebrating the new you who has grown strong. In the midst of a roadblock, obstacle, and detour, you have picked up and walked away from a crash without a scratch.

When we have allowed God to heal us, use us and stretch us many shifts take place, our energy picks up, our dreams become stronger and clearer, we will start to remember our dreams and begin to see revelations and confirmation throughout the day that confirm our gifts and assignments. This is where we stand in bafflement, faith, and excitement. You will find yourself less stuck and more directed, less the victim and more a unique and creative individual.

This is the result of not giving in or giving up, of moving on despite challenges of time, place or situation. This process of allowing God to stretch you and use you begets determination and tenacity to succeed in any area despite the mountain of insurmountable roadblocks, detours and obstacles. Stretching beyond your own capacity is the beginning of the breakthrough to freedom.

The shackles that I wore when being transported from prison to prison had the residue of trembling and trepid souls who gave up on life. In their view the shackles were placed on their minds and not their feet. Fears are imaginary. They are a product of your mind and do not exist in reality. They appear real but that is just an appearance. Just because I was cuffed and shackled did not mean that I was bound for life. It did not mean that my past or current situation determined my future.

What test have you encountered that mettle with your determination, and the endurance of your faith? What happened if many of our great leaders allowed fears to stop them from getting back up and moving forward?

What happened if Pres. Obama never ran for president because of his color?

What about Oprah because of her weight?

How about Malcolm X taking that trip that changed his complete view on the human race?

Let's look at Moses after seeing a burning bush? Or Harriet Tubman as a female slave? And the list goes on.

Every fear fighter and success warrior has scars. The Road to Redemption demands a drive and audacity to be different. It requires you to see past the shackles that have held you down in the past. It demands you to move past the "support" from those afraid to have an ardor for the unseen vision you have planted inside.

Fear cannot happen in your life if you don't give it permission. The more you conquer the more you accomplish, the more you accomplish the more you conquer. But you need a strategy and you need to stay focused.

Stretch your gift by writing it down. Writing your intentions with "Thy will be done" in the plan requires no special supernatural power. Do not over think your intentions write them without limitations, being frivolous and spontaneous. If you take the time to really think about what you are writing you will begin to limit yourself and the belief you have in God in endorsing your plan. Remember God is your source and you are in position to have an unlimited bank account, to have unlimited resources and unlimited ideas. During my time in prison, I had to learn that God is limitless and he can visit you wherever you are and deliver you wherever you are if you place no limitations on his power. We often unconsciously put a limit or range on how much God can give us or with what he can help us. We get real stingy with ourselves and selfish. Without even knowing it we often send God's gifts back when it is beyond our imagination or deserving.

Stretch your gift by recognizing that God is unlimited, not in a box, not in a building, he is everywhere waiting for you to free yourself and give yourself permission to use the gifts he has given you despite where you are and what you have. Many times he will have an unmarried person support married women, he might have a temporarily disadvantaged person speak in front of millionaires.

Cooperate with Gods plan and you can begin to let go of the self-sabotage. God has lots of money, many ideas, many jobs, many positions, and many houses. God has what we need if we just allow him to use the gifts he has given us. See I was caught up in being worldly, sophisticated, dignified, and smart, which is an immediate block for the flow of abundance. Behind bars proved to me that, gifts are all spiritual and require major leaps of faith.

Ask yourself: Am I avoiding my next step?

If you know this is your season to use what you have, watch how you spend your time and with whom you spend your time. Are you around people who can contribute to your growth? Are you around poisonous procrastinators and stubborn stagnators? Take in consideration that when you upgrade so will your associations. Many teachers and coaches say get rid of the toxic relationships, well what if you decided to bring your toxic individual with you to a conference, personal development seminar or to church? Instead of ditching them and having to deal with the same personality type or characteristic in your business or your job, how about turning the toxic relationships into transformed relationships. Now you have power of influence. You can be a positive influence to your toxic relationship individuals.

In case they do not wish to raise the bar and get in touch with reality, and wish to continue to harm you during your healing process, then let go and keep it moving, matter of fact let go and start running and do not look back. This is the start of your road to freedom. Freedom of mind, speech, creativity, love, and change.

Your road to freedom and success has nothing to do with your age, race, nationality, income, background, facebook fans or twitter followers. Once you declare it, do not worry about how to get to the land of more than enough. Your job is to act, set up, prepare, and be ready to show up and show out whenever an opportunity presents itself. Many of us miss the mark because we are consumed with our limiting beliefs, controlling EGOs, critics, being a perfectionist or just not being prepared.

Be prepared for your next level by putting on your crown of jewels, think royal, think big and do not stop. If you can grab your vision, you need a bigger vision. We are here to give birth, co-create, build wealth and legacies. Your life is a creation. It is a beautiful work of art. You are the artist and you can explore and define what you want to create. Do not be afraid to work your mojo, use what you have, perfect your skill and craft.

Are you ready?

Are you willing?

Are you able?

Like attracts like so that means success attracts success. The more you feel successful the more success will come your way. You cannot and will not feel successful if you first do not acknowledge your successes. The power of gratitude will turbo charge you to your next level. That is why it is important to be grateful for the progresses that you have made in your life. Gratitude is not a statement, it's a firm decision. It's a decision that we make to look past the apparent mountains and road blocks in our life and find the good and the great things that have happened. We have to condition ourselves to find the good even in the dreadful times. The key to the next level, the next destination on the Road to Redemption is constant gratitude. Then start to declare some things.

Declare your big vision

i.e. "I am a #1 NY Times best selling author

Declare a short term intention

i.e. "I will have a productive and prosperous day today"

Declare a supportive belief.

i.e. "Manifesting wealth, health, peace and joy is not a struggle. Poverty, sickness, and anger is."

Are you ready to raise the capacity of your mindset?

Are you willing to be grateful when all hell breaks loose?

Are you hungry enough to get crystal clear and in alignment?

The number one reason people don't get to their next level is that they don't set clear intentions. It is imperative that you know your objective. By doing so, you will engage your mind's RAS "Reticular Activating System". This is like pressure to a pipe. The RAS attracts and alerts you to opportunities which are in alignment with your intention. The RAS allows you to see God's gifts. The RAS is more than a sense of discernment but it prevents you from chasing after "what's next" to being receptive and alert when doors open up, when prayers are answered.

I love the prayer of Jabez for this specific reason. Jabez made it clear what he wanted and why. In the Bible the prayer Jabez said allowed God to be mighty because Jabez RAS was in alignment. "Jabez called on the God of Israel, saying, *'Oh that Thou would bless me indeed, and enlarge my coast [territory], and that Thine hand might be with me, and that Thou would keep me from evil, that it may not grieve me!'* And God granted him that which he requested." 1 Chron 4:10

Chapter 3:
A Little Hope Can Go
a Long Way

A ll successful leaders embrace their personal and professional life experiences. When looking at your current situation, what do you feel is holding you back? Is there something standing between you and the next level of achievement? That something may be one of your negative habits or limiting self-beliefs. Perhaps it is one small flaw or a behavior you barely even recognize. It may be an adopted characteristic that does not come from you. You will never reach palace thinking like a peasant. You must know that you are SOMEBODY even when no one cares. You are one of a kind and you should never be ashamed of what you are going through or what you have been through. Each experience is an opportunity for you to build a reservoir of faith in your ability to overcome and to push others to overcome. We must become teachers of teachers and leaders of leaders. There also requires a high level of follow-ship to go right along with your leadership position in the world. You are not a peasant, slave, convict, addict, homeless or anything else that is disempowering. You are unique and one of a kind. Your experiences may be similar to someone else's but we all walk out of the valley with a different life lesson.

Did you miss your lesson?

Are you holding yourself back from the most valuable keys to overcoming?

Let me share with you based on my experiences and observation, five things that hold some of us back from learning from our experiences.

- Passing judgment -- the need to rate others and impose our standards on them.
- Starting with a "no", "but", or "however". The overuse of these negative tone words are qualifiers, which secretly say to people, "I know it all" and "I don't care what you have to say", "I am right and you are wrong".
- Making excuses -- the need to reposition our negative behavior as a permanent fixture so people excuse us for it.

- Not listening -- this is Communication 101. The most passive aggressive form of disrespect is not listening and tuning the other person out, or dismissing the conversation, by weighing it for substance and relevance rather than tuning in with full attention.
- Fuzzy Vision -- not clearly communicating your vision. Why you do what you do, who you do it for, what does the business look like five years from now, ten years from now, thirty years from now?

Just as many entrepreneurs, I launched my business with an idea, okay, maybe two, okay maybe three ideas, little cash, and little experience. I had the degree, I had the passion but I lacked one major skill and that was the focus. My first "real" business venture was "Business In Progress Inc." I say the word "real" because my ventures that I engaged in before BIP Inc. were just hobbies.

I was what you would consider a hobbyist, a practitioner. Constantly testing the waters, trying to discover which business model worked best for me, and the lifestyle I wanted to live. BIP Inc. was demanding and time consuming. My partner and I worked long and hard hours for NBA and NFL athletes and several music artists supporting them in expanding their brand. BIP Inc. was responsible for writing the business plans, proposals and bridging the gap between the talent and corporate America to make a magical deal happen at the table.

The problem I had with BIP Inc. was that I was working a twenty-hour shift. Twelve hours at my job, two hours with my children and that included breakfast, dinner and pick up in total, one hour with my spouse and five hours with my business. The business was demanding and required long hours, several meetings at off hours and weekends, tons of dinner meetings, lots of traveling and the pay was slow. My motivation started to dwindle and I was burned out and mentally drained.

I struggled for months, reading books, attending seminars, conferences, networking events, working countless hours. My goal was to become financially independent and have the time to do what I want, when I want, and go wherever I wanted to go. The concern that I had, and most mom entrepreneurs have, is that we come with the million-dollar ideas, and we have the passion and drive to make them come to fruition but we do not ask for the big four-letter word, HELP, and we do not do the four-letter word REST.

On the *Road to Redemption* despite what venture you embark on you must have downtime, time to do absolutely nothing. Doing nothing will keep your hope levels high. Without it, the journey will leave you feeling vexed, stressed, confused, angry, and many times depressed. I call this taking a "pit stop". Either this is when you are forced to recharge or you take the time to become restored.

Many of us harbor the belief that work has to be work and not play, and anything that we really want to do or accomplish requires complication and difficulty. You know that saying, "I knew this would happen" or "just my luck" or "every time something good happens, something bad happens". This disempowering inner conversation starves our hope. To thrive we must be available and ready, not exhausted or burned out.

Keep hold of HOPE and do not let go. Once you accept that it is okay to be YOU, authentically YOU, flaws and all, you can begin to accept the fact that the creator, God will have whatever you need; whenever you need it, for your journey, your assignment including individuals who can help you with what you are doing.

Finally I decided that I needed a mentor to teach me, a team to implement and clients that would pay me more money without me compromising my time and my family. After several months of searching, observing, and being clear on what I needed to make this "real business" work, I met my business coach and the rest is history. My business started to shift, hope showed up just when I was ready to throw in the towel to support me in my dream.

I worked with my first business coach Andrew Morrison and was completely transparent about my life and my business, and it helped that he had a keen sense of discernment.

I worked closely with my coach for three years and who introduced me to the world of Virtual Assistants. Based on the problems I identified within the coaching, speaking and authors industry, I could niche my services for higher paying clients based on the demand for back-office support.

The struggle many of these individuals had was perfectionism. Many authors, coaches, and speakers were stuck in "getting it right" and could not focus on perfecting their craft. The perfectionism was a sign that they refused themselves the right to move forward. They were stuck, as many of us are at one point or another, with being obsessive in the debilitating system that keeps us stuck in the details and lose sight of the big vision.

How many times have you stopped yourself from doing something, producing something, or creating something freely? I say let the errors and mistakes reveal themselves later, don't stop yourself by focusing on all the details. Get a mentor to consult, get quiet to listen for instruction and hold tightly to hope. Do not fear failure, and do not be afraid of mistakes, there are none, only lessons. Lessons that will help you redeem yourself and connect you intimately with the goodness of God.

With the help of my coach, and the guidance from God, I could transfer my corporate skills to becoming a freelancing Virtual Assistant (VA), thus building outsourcing teams for small-business owners. I built a dream team of Virtual Assistants who were all stay-at-home moms with skills that Corporate America would die for but not pay for. I decided to expand and start training programs, coaching and consulting and created online memberships, showing other Virtual Assistants how to increase their business and niche themselves to make more money. Before I knew it, I was running a worldwide online organization for hundreds of freelancers, outsources and virtual assistants. I was then coaching the business owners on how to build sustainable business models while creating a unique selling proposition.

Business was so encouraging that I felt it was time for me to submit my letter of resignation.

That was one of the best decisions I made. My family thought I was crazy, but I understood that not everyone is going to understand and not everyone is supposed to understand my vision. That is what it is called MY VISION.

TAKE LEAPS IN THE DARK AND BE COURAGEOUS DURING THE DAY

After years of experience and working with hundreds of entrepreneurs, I began to make some revelations about my business and the keys to my success. I learned how to have courage when there were no windows and no doors; I learned to have courage when I was miles and miles away from home on a prison camp in Texas. I had courage when I wanted to get home early and agreed to go to boot camp to get out sooner than five years. I had to have courage when one of the prison counselors molested me in segregation because I wanted to make a phone call home or get an extra hour of recreation time. I had to use that same courage when my business was failing, when I left my children's father, when I became a single mother, when I knew without a shadow of a doubt that it was time to leave my job to pursue my dream that I talked about earlier.

Courage is what will pull you through the day and help you to take leaps in the dark when things do not look and feel so safe. Courage is the key to reinvention, redemption, having that personal and professional breakthrough.

I say all of this to say, I have accelerated because of my failures and learned the most valuable lessons from my mistakes. I have taken notes along the way and documented the roads that I should no longer travel down such as, the Road to Poor Me, the PITY PARTY and it leads to further frustration. Then there is the No Self-Esteem, forget low self-esteem, how about No self-esteem. This is the roadblock where many of us settle for less by selecting the road that leads to dead ends.

All the things I have survived, endured and accomplished, I could have let the inner critic reign supreme by telling me my life was useless because I was single mother, ex-con, still in school, tired of being tired, stressed from not relaxing and having to be strong all the time, sexually frustrated and spiritually disconnected. Whew…I could have considered myself a hot mess instead of a mess that was about to be blessed.

One of the most difficult tasks I had to face was survival. Surviving loss, loss of freedom, loss of money, loss of beliefs, and loss of faith. These losses are like sign post on our *Road to Redemption*, these losses in many ways turn into strengths. Losses should be celebrated and not mourned. We lose to gain something greater, so in all actuality you never lose you always win. The idea of losing is to survive, to learn how to let yourself move on, making a u-turn and getting back on course.
Every loss is a win, and every end is a beginning.

Again, I found myself in a familiar situation and I was uncomfortable because once again, I had settled for the fantasy life I dreamed about and accepted unnecessary abuse and violation that material trinkets offered. After my release with this newfound respect for myself and my life I was approached by a distraction that met me right where I was mentally. Do not be surprised when you have healed and gone through the first roadblocks, then a distraction presents itself which is set up for you to fall off course completely.

Well I came home to settle in for an emotionally and mentally abusive relationship. I was given the luxury cars, the mini mansion, the money, the diamonds and more. I had accepted less to receive more of temporary satisfaction. Years of stripping my confidence, hope, courage and faith sent me on a detour through a hopeless traffic jam as I became completely codependent on him and what he had to offer.

Many mentally abused individuals tell themselves they are not worthy of this, or cannot live without that most of the time they have been brainwashed to believe that it is too late to pursue their dreams, that they may look crazy if they say something, no one will understand what they are going through.

Breakthroughs happen in the moment when we pick up courage. Our egos are afraid of this courage because it means that we may do something bold, our egos try to play a trick on us from being started and revved. Instead of continuing the *Road to Redemption*, we focus on the length of the trip, what we have and do not have what we need and where we are going. The only thing you need to focus on at this point is the process and taking inspired action toward the original plan.

That was not my dream; my dream did not include any emotional, verbal, or mental abuse. I knew I had to alter my dream again and that I had to go back to the drawing board to write the vision and make it plain. I knew at this point that I had settled for less. Courage requires action, and this is not good news to most of us. Taking action means that we have to be responsible, and for some reason we avoid that at all cost. We want to blame someone, something or somewhere for our detour. Taking action means you have to do something to heal.

After five years of soul searching, you would think that I had learned my lesson of not settling and stick to the "overcoming" formula. When you feel as if you are taking one step forward and two steps back, remember it is a process. You have to monitor your thoughts and actions closely to avoid picking up anxiety along the way. It is easy for you to fall prey to anxiety in lieu of taking action steps to heal.

HAVE FAITH, OPEN YOUR EYES, PRAY YOUR WAY THROUGH, ENJOY THE PROCESS.

Pit Stop:

Activating your Hope means that you have strategies in place that help you go from the land of not enough to the land of more than enough. Life has many ways of putting a hold on us to mold us for our mission. From work related pressure, family stress, health issues, political discomfiture, and religious principalities.

What comes out of you when you are squeezed, watered, shaped, reshaped, pressed, pulled, molded, and formed? -- most likely, you will reek of the scent of "settling". Smelling as if you have showed up in guilt, envy, jealousy, unhappiness, frustration, anger, depression, fear, hate, embarrassment, sorrow, nervousness, shame, pride, ego, or doubt. This aroma is something you picked up during the process and have now gone from weeds, to stems, to branches. Your life strategy was to start a business and you suffered financially because you refused to believe in yourself enough to charge more, so you settled for less. Fear was a branch you grew. Your life strategy was to build a happy home and you were emotionally, physically or either mentally abused, so you settled for less.

Depression was another branch you grew.

When the strategy fails, you plan again, you set a new goal, you devise a clever way to accomplish and overcome. If we are to possess the land, why are you looking for a corner in the box?

If you believe that you are destined for greatness, why are you afraid to step out of your comfort zone? If you are intending to be grounded, why do you allow others to uproot you?

If you are waiting for your knight and shining armor to show up, why are you trying to change him into what he is not?

You must remember, remember, remember your thoughts, choices, and actions have power. You are not just a piece of flesh at the mercy of whatever life puts on your plate. You are a co-creator of the reality you live in. Life strategies only work if you work them. The next time you feel discouraged, or disempowered. Know that you are anything but powerless and never, ever, ever, ever settle for less.

Chapter 4:
They Call It a Comeback

A comeback is like recovering from an injury. We are more comfortable being a victim, the one lost on the journey because of a distraction rather than having to be consistently productive and proactive in our own lives. You might have to make a u-turn, you might have to stop at one of the pit stops to get your strength back, remember that the *Road to Redemption* is a process. The process is supposed to be fun, but it gets scary when the landmarks, roadside attractions are detoured by potholes, humps and bumps distract you.

Do not be ashamed to ask for help when you find yourself at the same rock in the road. For four years, I found myself in self-imposed exile with my children's father. I was going through u-turns and felt discouraged about my future. As I stated earlier the objective of the journey is to survive the obstacles.

Once we admit the need for help, guess what? Help shows up right at your door. The ego wants to stand on the pride of being "independent, need for no one, and self sufficient". Ask for help. Go ahead ask for it right now. I can bet you a dollar that you have been doing this all alone and not asking for help.

Ask yourself; whom can I ask for help? What kind of help do I need?

Look at nine of the blockages based on my observation that prevent most women from learning through their u-turns and detours.

- Comparing yourself to others
- Neglecting to ask for the four-letter word HELP
- Playing small, trying to dumb down our gifts
- Lacking awareness of your powerful impact on others
- Failing to cheer on the success of other women
- Shiny Object Syndrome
- Difficulty investing in yourself and your potential
- You circle of influence
- Perfectionism

Which of these common roadblocks are you making?

Your experiences are part of your pathway way to making a powerful comeback. It is the beauty of your song, the beauty of your life, flaws, and all. Somebody is waiting for you to take a stand, somebody is waiting to know who you are at a deeper level. Somebody is waiting for the lesson you can teach, the wisdom you can bring forth, the healing you can speak into his or her life. Your experience is power. Your experiences are what make you unique. This bridges the gap between who you think you are and who you really are.

The spirit and power of you is in you. It is called your comeback experience. You went through specific situations and circumstances for a reason. That reason is with you when you walk, when you talk, when you love, when you are just being you because you cannot help it.

I want you to repeat after me.
- I am powerful
- I am beautiful
- I am magnificent
- I am awesome
- I am standing in my power that God has given me.

LOVING YOUR FLAWS AND ALL

God has bestowed the power upon you to persevere, to overcome, to transform, to love, to give, to stand. Use your experience to get what is yours. As women and moms we do it all, for everyone, everywhere, however, whenever, for whomever, but the one person who needs it most. YOU.

We believe that the more we give of ourselves, the better we will feel, the better we will be as a mom, wife, follower, steward, sister, daughter, and so forth. This is far from the truth. Your experiences are about you valuing yourself, your power, your mystery, and your strength. It is the organic essence of who you have been, who you are not, who you want to be, and who you are right now.

We willingly give away our voice of experience, our voice of reason to make sure that somebody else receives what he or she needs -- but not after you finish with this book. You will learn how to use your voice, hope, and survival tactics to get out of your comfort zones out of the corner and speak your truth. On the *Road to Redemption*, you are going to begin to reap your harvest from all the work you put in.

Yes, I admit it is a process, but it is going to be worth it. All the growing up we had to do, the tears we shed, the healing and wound licking we had to do, the sleepless nights, the empty bed, only you and God. The only truth is in your powerful voice, flaws and all. We are going to activate our life with a new pep, in our step.

During this journey to the powerful comeback, you must leave the drama and resentment behind.

Resentment and drama are powerful drugs. When we focus on resentment and drama, we add poison to our process. When we are ogling the drama and resentment for others, we take our focus away from the road. We lose our sense of direction and we often receive the wrong directions. Resentment and drama lay at the root of many roadblocks. We must attend to what and where our inner guidance is nudging us. We cannot afford to think about who is doing what to whom, who is getting ahead of us and who deserves what or why we allowed this to happen to us again. The addiction to drama and resentment literally stops us in our tracks. It leads us away from our authentic selves into a defensive state of mind that places us outside the process and outside our circle of influence. We are now able to define ourselves and our journey based on someone else's.

Stop allowing people to joy ride and stop picking up hitchhikers along the way. Be willing to experience the rocky roads, be willing to upset people, somebody is going to get pissed off, somebody is not going to understand your calling, and some people are not going to support you. Stay away from the energy and power vampires, those people, or self-inflicting habits that want to suck the life out of you. These assigned distractions follow you around to misguide you and put you off course.

Your COMEBACK experience is the song you sing and the words of your soul. Write your song and sing it loud. Make your song a platinum hit. Live authentically. What God has for you is for you. Do not wish or want someone's success or life experience because you do not want what they did to get it, or what they have to do to keep it.

In my experience, I see women, who read noteworthy books that really motivate them and push them to act, but they get the information and they sit on their power, they never share their experience or their story. The motivation last a few weeks maybe even a month or so before "life" kicks in. As we continue to ease on down the *Road to Redemption*, we are going to pick up a few more tools to keep you focused. Now is the time to have a fierce conversation with yourself about what you are going to do differently after reading this book without getting caught up in the "compare and contrast" mindset. Focus on what it is within you that is struggling to be born. This is not a race; it is a consequential breakthrough necessary for a victorious shift in your life and direction.

Take a stand right here and right now, about your time, your spirit, your heart, your mind and most of all your voice.

With worth and past experiences use your voice. Somewhere along the trip, you gave up your voice. When you give up your voice you give up your power, you get off track. Get rid of the "nice girl syndrome". It is time to speak from the deep part of the belly within us from our ancestors. Stop allowing people to show up on your road to worthy inappropriately, stop allowing your circle of influence to hinder your experiences. Create clear boundaries.

My mother always told me to stand my ground by having a strong NO and a powerful YES, create clear boundaries, value yourself, and embrace your experiences.

"Be who you are and say what you feel, because those who mind don't matter and those who matter don't mind." Dr. Seuss.

Pit Stop:

Take life one bite at a time. We try to experience it all and speed the process up but the elephant has to be eaten one bite at a time. Are you hungry enough to go after what you want, tired enough of doing the same thing and following the same routine, pushed far enough in the corner to do something about the elephant on your plate?

Trust me it is not as bad as it seems. The elephant on your table may reflect a business you want to start, a book you want to write, a relationship you want to turn into a marriage, a new position you have been contemplating, credit that you need restored, or a relationship that needs mending.

The elephant on your plate can represent many things that you have ignored and brushed off, just to watch it grow bigger and bigger. The elephant is not going to disappear, so remember that, and save yourself some time and maybe some years. It is going to be there when you wake and when you go to sleep. When you try to drink or smoke it away or when you try to cry and sleep it off.

If it is your book, put together a writing schedule and stick to it. Invest in a hotel for a few nights and just work on your manuscript. That is what I will be doing next weekend. If it is mending a relationship, set some time aside to have that difficult conversation you have been avoiding. The most important thing to do when you have an elephant on your plate is to address the elephant and pursue the elephant. Some people have more than one elephant. You know it is there and you know it is not going to disappear, you may even know what you need to do.

Here are five simple tips to help you start chipping the elephant starting with the head.

- Name your "elephants."
- Select one and break it into bite-size pieces.
- Write these steps in the order in which they need to be completed.
- Assign start and completion dates for each item on your task list.
- Enter these dates into your calendar so you remember when it is time to do them.

As you focus on one bite at a time, you will be amazed at how this easy this process can get as you begin to implement it with every "elephant" in your life. Once you get the hang of this five-step process, you can now be free and along your way with an important decision, project or task you have been avoiding by taking the first bite to completion.

MAKE A DECLARATION

Repeat after me:

- I will receive what is divinely assigned and ordained for me.
- I declare and decree that everything, every vision, I put my hands on will prosper can be a blessing for someone else.
- I declare and decree that when I open my mouth to speak it will be a healing and blessing for someone else.
- I declare and decree that every talent, skill, and ability that I have will bring peace, love, and balance to those I encountered.
- In addition, it is so.

Your comeback experience calls for your essence to come forth, your strength, your potential, your unique beauty, your soft spirit, and your strong power, it's your song so baby it is time to sing it loud and proud.

Chapter 5: Take Your Time Walking Through the Valley

We are all on a spiritual quest to awaken our God given talents. It is important to develop a proper mindset and get a map for taking inspired action. This is not just taking action, but making sure that you move in a manner that produces desired results in your business, in your life, in your walk.

Taking inspired action prevents you from luring your dreams and racing through the valley. Walking through the valley will force you to accelerate change. Three fundamental concepts that help you in your dynamic transition and also assist in building a solid foundation.

FIRST CONCEPT IS RENEWING THE CREATIVE FIRE.

What are you intending to create. Why do you intend to create it? When you can identify and define your big WHY is only then you begin to get in alignment and on one accord with your purpose. When you identify the WHY, you stop chasing what seems to be the next-best thing and you begin to walk in your calling. Ask yourself WHY am I doing this? Why do I want to do this? Make sure your intentions are clear and your motives are pure.

SECOND CONCEPT IS RESTORING YOUR ENERGY.

Between time management and energy management, there is an important distinction. When you are on the go, living your life you have twenty-four hours to do what is necessary. That does not mean that you try to squeeze everything into one day. Spending your energy on what matters today to make a better tomorrow is the key. This is not about getting more done in less time, this is about aligning yourself to the vision and allowing the vision to activate you, motivate you, and energize you.

LAST, IS RAW REALITY.

Think of the bigger picture, with the results in mind. Redevelop how you see yourself in the next ten or twenty years. How can you begin to position yourself and your vision to create a generational experience? You are responsible for your vision. You are responsible for writing your mission; you are responsible for your goals. Write what your wealth plan looks like ten to twenty years from now. Begin to process your reality or rather the reality you are creating by thinking, planning and visualizing your dreams. With a telephone, laptop, and productive action plan, you could take over the world!

When walking through the valley, we have to look at how we are leveraging our time. How are you investing your time? Do not allow yourself to be defeated. Nothing can defeat you until it breaks your focus. My coach used to say the biggest sin is distraction. Work on what matters most until you execute it.

Now it is that time to read aloud these questions, write them, and think them through thoroughly before answering them.

- What are my priorities?
- What activities help me get greater results?
- What moves my vision forward?
- Why am I doing this?

- Who am I becoming?
- Whom am I affecting?
- Whom am I supporting?

On the *Road to Redemption*, you may need a different map of action steps and rest stops from others. You must experiment what works for you when overcoming your challenges and obstacles. Overcoming is a spiritual practice and a necessary process. It is not something that can be perfected, finished, put to the side, or given as a gift. It is my experience that we reach plateaus of overcoming challenges; however, we are often confronted with some valleys that are deep and dark.

We must become overcoming sharks. The ruthless truth is that some of us do not keep moving like the sharks we are, some of us sink to the bottom and give up. The decision we have to make and the choice is simple, we can pick up and begin again, to anew. We can become relentless and tenacious.

The process on the *Road to Redemption* is not a business, although you may reap many in-kind and monetary rewards. What we are after here is to support others by supporting ourselves, to lose the obsessive self-discovery and self-focus of exploring self. We have been fixated on self-improvement and self-empowerment. Our resistance to transformation is a form of self-destruction. We finish by throwing roadblocks on our own path. As we serve, we free ourselves from the narrow parameters of "me" to a boarder image of "them".

When dealing with inspired actions, you must get bigger than your to do list, bigger than your financial state, bigger than your living arrangements, bigger than your problems, bigger than your aches and pains, bigger than your thinking. A Bible verse compliments this chapter. Isaiah 55:8 says, "For my thoughts are not your thoughts, neither are your ways my ways, declares the LORD."

It is important for you to know that once you get out of your own way, you will allow God to move through you by expanding your territory and your vision. Taking action is essential, but there is more to this vision than just you, however big, bad, strong, and independent you are. Because no man is an island, you have to believe in something and someone, outside of yourself.

All high achievers, trendsetters and trailblazers believe in something greater than themselves. They believe in their families, they believe in their inner circle, they believe in their mentors, they believe in their causes, and most of all they believe in God! This is where inspired action becomes enrichment and fulfillment.

Now let us take look at that long to do list, is it enriching, fulfilling or inspiring?

- What does your "to do" list mean?
- Does it matter when you are in the valley?
- Will it move you forward while you are in the valley?

Do you have a positive action taking routine where three habits will push you forward and keep you out of procrastinating? Inspired action builds your confidence; the more confident you are, the more action you will take, and the more change you will make. The more you will learn while you are walking through the valley.

Invest one hour a day reading or listening to information that will support your personal or professional growth. What action step can you take today to move you from comfort zone to growth zone? Remember you do not get in life what you want; you get what you are and what you put in.

Here are two steps I want you to take as we move in the valley. The first step is to decide what you want and the second step is to believe you deserve what you desire then some.

- Get on purpose
- Be willing to fail
- Be willing to upset people
- Somebody is going to be pissed off
- Somebody is not going to like what you are doing

- Somebody is not going to understand your calling
- In addition, some people are not going to support you on your path

Pit Stop:

Here is a letter that I want you to tear out of the book and place on your whiteboard.

Dear Self,
I love you today!
I honor you today!
I value my time today!
I respect you and others today!
I am growing stronger today!
I am expecting a miracle today!
I am on time today!
I am prepared today!
I am using my creativity to shine today!
I am focused today!
I am showing up in the world differently today!

Signed_____

In my experience, walking through the valley meant that I had to make my inner light shine forth to direct me and to guide me. Being extradited from NY to Chicago, then from Chicago to Texas was not a pleasant ride. Shackled hands and foot, trying to walk without bursting into tears was just the beginning. Being transferred from state to state just to reach your destination meant that you were less than uncomfortable -- you were treated like an animal.

Walking in the valley meant that I had to remove any thoughts of my previous life and focus on survival. Walking in the valley meant that I had to rely on a higher power to get me through this, because "this too shall pass". Yes walking in the valley means some unpleasant things, such as embarrassment, humiliation, ego crushing, pride breaking, and character building will happen to you. Yes, character building. Out of the valley was a character and personality, hidden and pushed to the back burner, because the world was moving fast and I felt I needed to catch up. In this situation, I had no hold on time, no rush to go anywhere but to my destination so I can exhale and mix my formula of HOPE up again. Besides building character, I built leadership skills better than the executives on Wall Street did, I have a PhD in leadership from the school of Hard Knocks, and a certification in life coaching from all the women I listened to, monitored, evaluated from afar, to see how they coped in these unfortunate circumstances.

I had to affirm to myself with energy and conviction, "I can do this, I will get through this". I watched how many of the women confronted their fears. I am not talking about confronting other women; I am talking about dealing with their limited beliefs of themselves. It was like a regurgitation process. Everyone was releasing and coping with whatever happened to them from five years old and up. Everyone had no choice but to face their life, their fears and their beliefs head on and so did I. After 2 years I finally gave in that there is never a good time, no better time than right now. There is no better place than right here. This was the place and the space for me to release all feelings of bad timing, bad luck and bad genes and consider that I have what it takes to be somebody regardless of my now situation and the other consideration was that no one was going to do it for me. I had to heal on my own and everything I need to heal is already within me.

Chapter 6:
I Found Something on the Inside

My life is a result of my thinking. Everything I created, manifested, and positioned myself to receive is all on ME and in ME. If you are not happy and satisfied with your current state it is time to shift, change and reprogram. Placing ourselves around positive people, places and things will make life a lot easier for us. Creation is our second nature, so when it seems difficult to create, complete goals, and manifest our visions, perhaps we are allowing outer sources and forces to condition us to accept and be complacent with our current state.

How many times have you put yourself on the back burner? How many times have you stood for yourself and put your needs, wants, and desires first? If we are in the miracle manifesting business, we can no longer do things "their way" or allow ourselves to revel in the "pity party" or "playing the victim." Look at your inner circle. Are they givers or takers? This has a lot to do with who comes first. Most of the time we do more for the takers in our lives than the givers. We make excuses for the takers, we spoil the takers and we inform the takers on our next move so they can take some more. The givers we ignore, the givers we connect with now and then, we call on the givers when the takers suck us dry. If you are in the business of manifesting miracles then you have to put God first.

The manifestation of miracles happens every day, all day. We have joined for one specific miracle. It should be on our mind all the time. We must be prepared to take full advantage of it and know how to maximize on it, so we can be able to bless ourselves and be a blessing to someone else. For example, we ask for money, we get it, and then we do not do the right thing with it. We ask for help, and when it comes, maybe not from whom we wanted it, we deny it or receive and do not appreciate it. We ask for health, but we continue to poison our bodies, we ask for a new position, but we complain that we hate our jobs and the girl that sits next to us.

Look at the blessings and miracles you have received in the past. Did you make the best of it, did you really appreciate it, or did you fulfill a temporary satisfaction? Giving is one thing and taking is another.

Write down a positive affirmation, post it on your bathroom wall, place a copy in your journal, and place one in your purse or wallet. Look at it at least eleven times a day. Write an affirmation as if it already happening. Avoid using "I want to do" or "I want to get" in your affirmation. Use action words, words of power such as "I am" "I will".

What I found within was a place to pay it forward and place to make small contributions to the world. This I call Bank of Unlimited Resources. Making small deposits into the Bank of Unlimited Resources will always open doors to new opportunities and miracles.

I had a conversation with one of my clients and she talked about how she was finding it hard to stay above water financially. With worry and fear in her voice, I can hear the root of the problem. Her problem stemmed from months and years of resentful giving, and people pleasing. She was surrounded by takers. Many of us give from a mentally and physically exhausted, and maybe even financially tapped out stance.

As the conversation, continued clarity began to show its face. Quick note: "Always say to God in a silent prayer "Let there be light" during the conversation or before the conversation. This breaks down any barriers. "

When it comes to giving, in my opinion it is important to give in order to change someone's situation, circumstance or well being. Many of us give to the point where we handicap a person's capabilities to think and do for themselves. This causes a lot of energy to be dispersed and sometimes finances being depleted.

When I am being used as a blessing or paying it forward, I feel as if I am making a small deposit into the Bank of Unlimited Resources. For example, when my children need something, resources show up, when my mother takes the trip to the doctor for a test result, good health shows up, when my kids need to go to college, scholarships will show up, when I am low on funds, contracts show up, when I am looking for a breakthrough for a client, answers show up, when I feel discouraged, someone has a kind word for me to keep me going. Super natural resources will show up without me begging, pleading or worrying because I know I have made deposits into the Bank of Unlimited Resources and I wake up knowing that I have another opportunity to be a blessing to someone TODAY.

As for my Incubator client, she was able to focus on what she was giving others and why. She was able to identify the money making opportunities in her business by getting focused. This was a major shift for her to be able to pull out a withdrawal from the Bank of Unlimited Resources. She was able to identify what she needed in order to grow her business, save her marriage, say "no" to some family and friends. Three days later, she called me with a major client project and the baby sitting support she needed for her children as well as making a date to spend time with her husband.

Life can be rewarding. Give from what's inside. Knowing that you are dealing with the Bank of Unlimited Resources, the opportunities are limitless.

"MY PERSONAL AFFIRMATIONS"

_____

_____

_____

_____

_____

_____

_____

_____

_____

_____

_____

_____

_____

_____

_____

_____

_____

_____

_____

_____

_____

_____

Chapter 7:
Every Season Has a Gift

Physical, financial, spiritual, and emotional challenges are real. They create boundaries and obstacles in our lives. However, guess what? We can move beyond boundaries, challenges, and obstacles. Look at your life, it reflects your beliefs, the inner beliefs are what really do the mojo on you. Those are the beliefs that are injected in us as children such as (hard work pays off, we have to struggle, hard to find a good man, not thin enough, not light enough, not smart enough, being just right, just making it, not holy enough, never enough).....according to some of our beliefs that we have flowing in our veins like blood.

You may know this but, what you believe is the foundation of what you do and do not do. I want you to write one belief that has been hindering you from being (enough for God). Stop living for everyone else, being what others see you as, if it is not your authentic self. You are more than enough for God and you will serve a disservice to your destiny if you do not change your beliefs about yourself. You will begin to infect your children, your family, and your friends with your beliefs that are false.

Misery does not need company, stay clear of people who want to litter in your ear. We are carrying precious cargo (book ideas, business, ministries, professions, and so on) stay clear from anyone who will not support in the growth process. Stay clear of vampires who just want to break you or your idea's down.

Write your ideas in your journal. Do you want to write a book? (Pick a title) Do you want to start a business? (What kind) Do you want to leave your job? (Write a resignation letter and put a date on it) Do you want to increase your finances? (Open a separate bank account from where you normally dip in to pay bills)

Les Brown stated that the richest place is the graveyard, I say the richest place is the prison, there are so many undiscovered talent that is not being utilized and not exposed, in capable bodies. So much talents sitting there waiting for a 2nd chance. When it comes to reducing recidivism there was no program in place. You are stripped of your name you are labeled a number, when you come out and into civilization you are monitored like an animal-tested product, you are labeled a high risk, you are marked as a "problem" before anyone discovers who you really are and what you can do. You are constantly challenged to prove that you can fit in society; you constantly have to prove yourself as a "good girl".

Then there is the sympathy where everyone is careful with handling you, and they place FRAGILE on your forehead. The truth is I was fine, many of the people I encountered in the halfway house when I got home were sane. "Society" was losing it. I was at peace, excited to conquer the world, excited to utilize my underperformed assets. I was meditating daily, I was reading my word, and I was connected to life and was ecstatic about my future. I was "happy" and full of "joy", not because of where I came from but because of the experience and process I been through. A transformation process, time to reflect on the real, unscripted, and unrehearsed self. A transition process that took me from self-righteous to standing on God's word. I had experienced God at a level that was incomprehensible to the "religious" folks out in the world. It was an intimate relationship and it kept me from losing my mind, it freed me when the doors were double and triple locked.

In this season, there was a gift of true love and peace of mind but you must stay focused, determined and willing to act.

Pit Stop: Get F.D.A Approved

Every time you begin to face a new project, venture, or idea, there are three things that you must make sure are in effect. Write this and remember these three words. Focus, Determination and Action.

When I started to interview women for my book, I had one thing in mind -- to discover the secret sauce in this mixture of women that has increased their vision to a successful journey. At the end of every interview, there were three important words that one must have or know and make habitual. Staying Focused, Being Determined, and Taking Action.

During your transition and transformation process, there will be some of you who experience "ah ha" moments, some will experience shifts and changes, some will experience separation, some will experience the past showing up, calling us, some of your fears will show its ugly face, some will experience a reality check, some will experience an altitude adjustment, some an attitude adjustment, and some will experience humility or integrity. Whatever you experience, whatever happens, whatever you begin to go through is an opportunity for you to grow through. This is a grow-through experience.

Take what you see, what you hear, and what you experience to sharpen your senses. We want to hear like a bat, see like a hawk, smell like a shark with these senses increased we can enjoy life as a process of growth and change to which we can adjust.

For example, with remarkable hearing, we can hear past a person's words, we can go beyond the conversation and into the core and root of what is really being said. With remarkable sight, we can look past a person flaws, not viewing others as manipulators or mischievous, we see them as children, frightened children who have been neglected, put out, looking for a way to grow; we will see problems as opportunities. With remarkable smell, you can smell the direction of the road on which you are heading. Dogs smell trouble before it comes, sharks smell their surroundings, (safe, unsafe, friend, foe or food), with a remarkable sense of smell you can smell a blessing in the air. You can smell how someone's spirit is ill or how someone spirit is sweet. It is all in the aroma and we all have a smell, some of us stink, some of us are musty, some of us smell sweet. I know you have heard that saying, "She's walking around like her s--t don't stink" or "smells like trouble". Well let us increase the sense of smell to direct us.

What you see determines what you experience, what you hear determines what you need to learn, what you smell determines what path you are on and in what direction you are headed.

Take ssome time over the next couple of days and think about having a difficult conversation with someone. Your mom, dad, spouse, partner, sister, brother, and so forth. The reason for this difficult conversation is to release some things, to clear your path even more. We have to confront and heal from specific situations. It was not until I had a difficult conversation with my family that a door opened for me – a door that I did not even know was a closed door.

Pit Stop: Let us get started. Ready, Set, Go!

I have a dream, he said
I am going to host my own talk show, she said
I have an invention, they said
Let us sell these cakes to the community, they said
Let us start a singing group, they said
I have an idea for people to communicate on the go
I would like to see this show on color TV
Let us try this medicine to see if it will save your life
I am the first female to...
I am a bestselling author
I am going to be an actor on the big scene
I am getting married
I am going to learn how to read

What do these statements share? No, guess again, almost. They are ACTIVATING their season. When you ACTIVATE your season, you go farther than you ever imagined. It does not take much to motivate and empower someone, but to ACTIVATE your season means that you are willing to take consistent action toward achieving personal success in life.

YOUR CIRCLE OF INFLUENCE MAY BE A SQUARE

Not everyone can go with you to your next level. Some people you will have to leave at the curbside to catch another bus. Make sure you fill your bus with people who can help you when the bus over heats, breaks down, needs gas, pray you through, know when to get off and understand that you are moving to a new destination.

I would like you to write everyone in your Circle of Influence. Lawyer, friends, doctors, family, cousins, BFF's, boyfriends, girlfriends, and so forth... Write the name of everyone who surrounds you and pick the people who are going to be supportive on the bus ride as opposed to those who will take up space and may sabotage the trip because of the position they hold. Some people you are going to piss off because they are going to wonder why you have lil Joey with you in the front seat of your bus and they are in the middle row. This is about your circle of influence and the position they hold in your life right now.

You are positioning yourself for success. Those people in your circle can weigh you down and make the journey longer than it should be, speed it up to where you are not prepared to brake and you and you end up crashing or help you pace yourself and reach the destination safe and sound.

I am on the road to success and my circle of influence helps me be Mrs. Activate. They are supporting me to be more, do more and have more. Check your circle; check your bus, which is in the wrong seat on your road to success.

Look at your inner circle and see whom needs a seventy-two-hour eviction notice. Start drafting your notices this week. We cannot move in action if we allow squatters to take up valuable space.

As people on the move, people in action, people of power, we have to be careful whom we allow to stay and occupy space in our home, our minds, our businesses, our relationships, and our life in general. We allow people to fill vacancies that need to be left alone. We are growing and need room for abundance and prosperity.

I barely watch TV but I turned it on and wanted to see what the big hype was about with this new show called Hoarders. Well to my surprise that was one of the worst and gross shows that I have ever seen. These people have allowed the past and the present situations and circumstances to cloud their minds and their homes. They allowed so much stuff to pile up externally that the real work of internal healing was necessary.

Many of those hoarders were covering space with things, and people around them have just adjusted to the lifestyle and did not attempt to make any changes. They are worse off than the hoarders are themselves because they were taking up space as well.

Let us begin to flush out and clean up the mess that is inside and outside of us. I always direct the question back to myself. Where can I begin to clean up in my life? What do I need to do to get my business in order? What is clouding my path to success? Is it my inner circle that is taking up space like a squatter or my outer circle, which are people who I feed into more than I feed into myself? How much longer am I going to allow people, things, and past situations take up space in my life?

If you have BIG dreams and aspirations, and you know you have a destiny to fulfill you must begin within. I repeat you must begin within. To whom do you need to give a seventy-two-hour notice? Could it be you? – Or getting out of your own way, your friends, your family, your spouse, or your job?

Think about it and begin to hand out notices that in seventy-two hours you will no longer have room for squatters.

Chapter 8:
Feast on Faith
and Fast on Fear

The *Road to Redemption* requires affirmative action. Many people are not accustomed to thinking about God's will for us and our dreams and visions. We often feel as if we should be dutiful and not bountiful. During our journey to overcoming life's challenges, obstacles, and detours, we must learn to keep our own counsel, to move slightly among critics and doubters, to voice our plans only among our believers and allies, and to be clear on who is praying for us or preying on us.

Hold your intention within yourself and stock up on power so you can manifest and produce. Count your blessing and feast on faith.

People talk so much about fear these days that is has become a convenient excuse just to sit in the corner and not act. Fearing should not be a fad and it is not cute, as my mother would say. Giving your power away to fear is like a lion giving up his position in the animal kingdom. Its normal and human in nature to be afraid of the unknown, but do not let it dominate you.

Life does not reward quitters, towel throwers, or forfeiters. If a lion does not conquer his fear, he will not be able to hunt the wild game; he would die of hunger all because he is afraid. So how does the lion conquer his fear, he goes after the big game. Game that is bigger and sometimes faster than he or she is.

We must be like the lion and roar, stop rattling like a snake and roar like a lion or lioness. Lions are extremely social and live in families called prides, notice the word pride. They are among other fearless lions. When you observe a lion in nature, you will notice that it is best described by its strength, natural dignity, and demand for respect. The lion is born as a powerful creature and power naturally comes to it. You attract what you are!

Each of us was not born with fear in us, it is something we decided to adopt. We told ourselves that fear can conquer us, shake, rattle and roll us around. You must remember your birthright. You are born powerful, fearfully and wonderfully made, just as the lion.

Get your roar back by doing the following:

- Hold your head high – even in times of conflict – conduct yourself with dignity and demand respect
- Stand tall, remember your birthright of power is moving through you always
- Showcase your authority (not by dominating and being arrogant) but lead others with a loving heart, love conquers all
- Protect your pride, stand for what you believe in, protect your vision, and be aware of enemies and friendemies (friends that really do not like you).
- Have courage to act and move when needed.
- Have faith

No matter what you have been through that may be paralyzing you, no matter what traumatic experience you have encountered now or in the past. We are all fearful of something, someone, or somewhere. However, you cannot sit there blessed with some gifts and you choose to paralyze yourself. You are cheating the pride from having a strong powerful leader; you have to go from crawling to walking at some point, so why not stand tall NOW.

Your past can and will unlock your future when you feast on faith and fast on fear. The promises you made in the past and the commitments you make in the future are surrounded by fear, but the seed that is planted is one of faith. Stick to your faithful commitments without fearing HOW things will be done.

How many commitments have you made to yourself? How many promises did you make that you never kept. This does not include anyone but you. Do you have unfulfilled commitments and promises that you made to yourself and did not keep? Why? If we can go all the way, back to the promises we said we would make and the commitments we said we would fulfill, we can write a book on it.

What makes the promises and commitments that you make today valid? What is different now that you will make an effort to be true to you and make sure your word is your bond to you. If you say you are going to do something for yourself or with yourself, what makes the person you are today a person of his/her word.

I am going to ask you to stop cheating yourself. Look at what we ask for then when you receive it you ask for it to go away. For example, the house you are in, the relationship, the job, and the friends you have. We sometimes are caught up in the "asking" and not the consequences of "having". Please God if you do this for me, I promise I will do ....,

God if you can help me get this job I promise I will ..... All I need is just one more chance, if you can get me out of this jam I promise I will....

Well guess what; many times the "I" will never be fulfilled. Your past holds the keys to your future.

- What were the circumstances or events in your childhood, when you gave up your power? You let someone or something influence you not to do what you wanted to do for you.
- Which of your personality traits or characteristics has caused things not to work out? The fear you might have, the Ms. Know it all attitude, being a perfectionist...
- What are the secret dreams or visions on which you have given up? Think about what you once loved to do and have stopped doing it for whatever reason.

Remember you have a choice to change your future today. Start by making a weekly focus calendar and start to make small daily commitments toward a specific goal. Map each day and write what step you will take that day to get closer to your goal. Monday you make phone calls, Tuesday you may go to a networking event or fellowship meeting, Wednesday you may do some online research ...Start small to make it big.

IT IS TIME TO BE HELD ACCOUNTABLE.

This is a no excuse zone; we can no longer blame others for our slack or lack or getting, doing or being something. Today we are accountable for our actions toward our success. In my experiences, having an accountability partner helped me complete many of my goals. Connect with an accountability partner for the next thirty days.

The goal of having an accountability partner (A.P) is to have someone help you reach your goal; help motivate you stay focused and help you grow. Make sure they are goal minded, serious about their personal or professional growth.

Once you connect, do the following:

- devise a confidentiality and nonjudgmental verbal agreement
- write in your journals about your progress and your next steps
- write your (A.P) progress and next steps
- commit to meeting consistently once a week or more if you choose

As an (A.P) accountability partner, you are responsible for putting the fire under your partners butt. Remember this is a No excuse zone.

Share the following:

Your thirty-day goal. Ask your (A.P) to hold you accountable to the "BEING as opposed to DOING" part. For example, I am Ms. Activator, as Ms. Activator I should be creatively activating everyday throughout the day, spreading my attribute like a disease, and infecting others with my inspiration. People should see nothing but activation, because that is who I am. How can I be an activator? By encouraging others, supporting others, making sure I give people I encounter a wow experience through my consultation and through my actions.

"WOW"

Pit Stop: Have a Drink of Boldness

Do something BOLD

Give and do what you want to be and have. It is easy to fall into fear, holding yourself back, feeling uncomfortable when it comes to do something or say something BOLD. In being bold, here are a few things to think about:

- Be your authentic self
- Tell someone how much you appreciate them
- Tell someone YES
- Learn to say NO
- Sit back and do nothing
- Love yourself (take yourself out on a date)
- Let go of toxic relationships, friendships, ships in general (lol)
- Ask questions
- Confront your demons (fear, self-doubt, low self-esteem, and so on.)
- Travel somewhere out of town or local, get out of your familiar territory
- Forgive someone in person (mom, dad, sis, brother, friend, and so forth.) remember no one is obligated to do you right or do you wrong.
- Try a new restaurant
- Join a support group/ church/ network
- Admit your wrong

- Go to the doctor or dentist
- Identify and embrace your fears (if you are scared of heights, go visit the Empire State Building)
- Treasure your relationships
- Use your senses learn to FEEL. (Many of us have blocked this sense and use it only when we want to, but learn to FEEL and let go do not put up a wall.)
- Go to an event or host one yourself
- Have a baby (lol. hahahaha. just joking, just wanted to make sure you were paying attention)
- Commit to do one BOLD thing this month.

FINISH WHAT YOU STARTED

During the halftime in a game, the entertainment comes out, the players get a rest, the coach reviews the game plan and motivates the team, a discussion happens about who is not performing at the highest and best, and whether they need more defense. Plenty of activity takes place during halftime that motivates the players to finish the game with intentions to win.

If your intentions are to win, win, win, no matter what, then moving past the halftime to the finish line is important. Beginning a new thing, a new project, a new pursuit is exciting. You have the result in mind, you see the long lines, the balloons, and the media at your launch, you count how much money you will have from the hundreds of people who sign up, you see yourself sitting on the stage with Donny Deutsch from the Big Idea. Here is the kicker, what many people do today is begin with a powerful start with all intentions to finish and stop right at halftime.

What happens when starters get to the halfway mark is; distractions, interruptions and the shiny object syndrome hinder starters making it to the finish line.

They no longer see themselves at the finish line, they are tired and overloaded, they are now feeling forced to stick to the plan, they are not completing deadlines, and are in a state of procrastination. The plan that involved those getting to the finish line has been intercepted.

If you are at halftime in your life, focus on finishing what you started. Take this time to look at the game plan and see what needs to be changed, added, or omitted. How you started may not be the way you finish, those who started with you may not be there when you finish. That is why halftime is so important.

Make a plan, work your plan, and you will attain your goal. Rely on your halftime strategy, planning, and process, not your willpower. You want to create a mindset and working environment (associates, partners, volunteers, advisers) that will pull you and push you forward toward the finish line.

Answer the following questions:

- What do you need to do to stick to the plan?
- What is the outcome you desire?
- What will it look like when you have attained the desired result?
- What will it feel like when you have reached your goal?
- With whom will you be celebrating or sharing this moment?
- Where will you be sharing the moment?
- How will your life differ from the way it is now when you cross the finish line?
- What aspects of your life do you have to overcome or change to cross the finish line?

If you want to stay motivated to complete what you have started, to move past halftime, then you must do one thing. Celebrate. Celebrate during halftime; congratulate yourself at that midway mark. This will heighten your motivation and determination to stay the course on your *Road to Redemption*.

Chapter 9:
Super Size Me

I know we have been through a trying and tested year, some had a prosperous year, some accomplished some goals, and others have started to step out of their comfort zone. In the end, we must look ahead at what we can do to make the coming year a glorious one.

How can we **UP LEVEL AND UP GRADE** our life-styles? How can we begin to work on building a closer relationship with those we love including ourselves? I can speak for myself when I make this statement that being a mom and being a mom with a business is both rewarding and discouraging at times. The emotional roller coaster that we ride during the growth and learning process of being a mom and being an entrepreneur has its highs and lows.

I encourage you to stay the course, keep driving, and do not give up. I do not care what life may look like right now or what your business looks like right now, we cannot continue to operate without truly **BELIEVING we can do it.**

A coach, consultant, conference or seminar, webinar or workshop, boot camp or training cannot equip you for the journey, these are just fuel for the ride, but you have to want success, you have to want to be free, have to want love and support.

T. D. Jakes would say, "Can you stand to be blessed?"

We are each a unique work of art, skillfully crafted, and created. Our lives are like a story, and with the power of free will, we can change the story. Each of our stories is different and our Road to Redemption may vary. Remember that you must have clear intentions. Do you want to create greater life balance, identify your lifework, clarify your unique skills, and implement actions that will move you closer to your divine passion and purpose?

With your intentions, I would like you to focus on Being present in your life as opposed to Doing more in your life.

Start a revolution beginning with you. Sow your seeds to someone today. A good word, a meal, a piece of clothing, a bottle of water, and so on... sow into someone else's life today

THE POWER OF SILENCE

In silence the power moves, things begin to shift, change begins to happen, truth is revealed, prayers are answered, ideas are manifested, dreams are made a reality, businesses are birthed and life finds its value in you then you begin to see your authentic self. Make time for dedicated prayerful silence, rest, reflection, and renewal. Focus on "Whatever is true, whatever is honorable, whatever is right, whatever is pure, whatever is lovely, whatever is of good repute, if there is any excellence and if anything worthy of praise, dwell on these things" (Philippians 4:8)

Move past the inner chattering mind. Invite an experience of peace that comes from stepping away from the selfless conversations. Give God space to speak, welcome him in. Be present when the spirit of the Lord is speaking to you. Follow the four Cs COMMUNICATION: Listening to God, COMPREHENSION: Understanding what God says. CONFIDENCE: Trusting in what God is doing, CHANGE: Being transformed by the word of God.

To have a constructive conversation with God, it takes two. You must be able to hear the questions he ask you and the instructions he provides. If we are too busy leaning on our own understanding and having unproductive conversations, we may miss the landmarks he gives for us to arrive at our destination.

The Bible tells us to meditate on God's Word. Our thoughts determine our behavior and what we think about is important. Do not miss the message by tapping in to the wrong source, tuning in to the wrong station, and turning off spiritually.

Here are three times during the day that you can tap in to, tune in to, and turn on to God's Word. Before you go to sleep at night, make sure that you have God's Word be the last thing that occupies space in your mind. When you wake, before you hit the ground running, start your day with God's Word, let that be the first thing to occupy space in your mind in the morning. Dedicate a specific time each day to be in God's Word so it can speak to you throughout your day, try lunchtime or after work.

Opening up your mind and increasing your mental capacity will Super Size you and your vision. We must have the power of love and not the love of power in us. The power of love is peaceful and forceful, the love of power is dominating and controlling. Let's avoid any pot holes during our journey that may cause us to have a flat tire and stop at the wrong pit stop.

Pit Stop: You are Under Arrest!

First degree of selling yourself short by not loving yourself just the way you are.
One count of lack of confidence
Two counts of low value proposition
Four counts of not planning
In short, why not you trust yourself or God for your success?
You may be afraid of success and of change. Can you live up to your standards of excellence? If you can, check two.
Do your loved ones support you? If yes, check three.

If you answered no to any of these questions, then you have some fixing to do. If your resume/bio really does not reflect who you are and what you can do, rewrite the resume/bio until it does. You may never need to send this resume/bio to anyone, particularly if you own your own business, but it is there to remind you that you are a "can do" person.

If you cannot live up to your standards of excellence, maybe the standards need changing, not you. Being a perfectionist is a two-edged sword. On the one hand, you do good work, but on the other, you keep tinkering because it is not quite right yet. Stop tinkering. It is fine.

If your loved ones are not supporting you, sit them down and explain your dreams and goals until they do understand

and get on board. Let them know how much time the business will take at first, but in the end everything will be OK. Tell yourself this too.

When you get past these obstacles, you will feel good about yourself. You will realize that you have what it takes and you are all that and a bag of chips. You just have to figure out if this is your go full speed season or patience is a virtue season.

Wait For It

Can you tell when you are being called to be patient and when you are called to act?

There will be those situations where you will question what to do? -- or what is next for me? Then you will question should you be patient, passive, make a move, who should you call what should you do.

The answer will not come until you get still. You must stop before you make a move. Not until you stop, look and listen will you receive guidance, divine guidance. Only then will you walk in the right direction, get a clear view of who to call, or know when it is time to act.

Be Still and Be Patient for Divine Guidance.

Chapter 10:
Be Faithful To Your Vision

On March 9th 2000 I was released from Federal Prison in Texas. When they say everything is big in Texas they are serious. The food was big; I have never seen ribs so big in my life. I stepped out of LaGuardia airport with a destination to return to a Halfway house for 16 more months. I was sad, but free. Tired of folks telling me what to do, but free. I just got off the plane and took the biggest deep breathe ever. I touched the ground and kissed the dirty NYC Street. I have a 2nd chance is all I could think of. I had $26 in my pocket, some street clothes and real sneakers. They call them tennis shoes in Texas. All I wanted to do was to go home to lie in my mom's bed, but the reentry process was just beginning and I was headed to another 4 walls with a fold up mattress.

Upon my arrival I took out my vision book that I have been journaling in and writing my business plans on and I sat there and just cried. I had the opportunity to complete my vision. I had a 2nd chance to go to college this time and stay there. The opportunity to use this new mindset that told me "I have what it takes".

After I served my time in the Halfway house, I was placed on probation. I could go home but had to be home whenever the phone rang from that famous 212 number. Five years of probation. Back and forth to the government to tell all my business and dare not to leave any of it out. What are you doing? Who are you doing it with? When are you doing it? Why are you doing it? The complete drill year after year. I had my share of Facebook before it was even launched. My face was an open book for the government and anyone else who needed to know my "ex-con" status. As a young girl in her twenties I had a curfew and I had to fill out a daily pass that explained my whereabouts down to when I go get my hair done, to what time I will go to Burger King, to the time I will get on the train and how long will the job interview will take. It was tedious and it was not what I call rehabilitation or re-entry support. At one point I just wanted to go back and do the rest of my time instead of being teased with freedom.

Through it all I held on to my vision and as life moved on, my position in life progressed. I was a mom set to be a mom entrepreneur. I pursued my vision and completed most of my goals in the vision book by the time my probationary period ended, some goals changed and others were marked "done".

I started as most mom entrepreneurs, frustrated with my job, wanting to pursue my dreams, make more money, and do what I wanted to do, when I wanted to do it, and however I wanted to do it. I rebelled and left Mr. Corporate America to see if I could make it without him. It has been more than seven years now and I have not returned. I now have the freedom and flexibility I craved. On the business front, I deliver inspiring keynotes, coach women business owners, and mompreneurs. On the home front, I am able to enjoy my family and play with my little 9mth old at the mommy and me events during the week.

I do not know about you, but the relationship I had with Mr. C (Corporate America) was abusive.

He kept me from my children, kept me from my friends and family, and most of all kept me from being me. Mr. C made it clear that he wanted fifty years of my life. He never really acknowledged my talents and in fact, he did not care. He told me I could only be sick a few times a year, I could eat once a day when he said so. He told me what to wear, how to talk, and when to talk. He gave me money every two weeks, just enough to survive and told me that I had to show up rain, sleet, hail or snow. I will never forget the day he told me that I could only take fourteen days out of the year, and had the nerve to call it a vacation...

I have been tempted to cheat on my vision when times were rough -- when I suddenly became a single parent with two small children, when my lights were turned off, when my computer crashed while working on a client's thirty-page business plan, when my car was towed for tickets, not once, not twice but three times for more than $1000 each time, only because the signs in the city were hard to read, when all I wanted to do was attend a networking event free. In the midst of it all, and despite it all, I had to believe that I was going through a process of preparation.

When Mr. C came knocking at my door, with flowers and candy, with new positions and promotions, I had to stand firm on my decision and make this thing called VISION work. I needed to hang around visionaries, listen to visionaries, and eat with visionaries who were not my peers, but at a level that I wanted to reach.

You will be tried, tested, and tempted when it comes to your Vision. When the going get rough, when the roads get rocky. Are you willing to wipe off the dust, dry your eyes and keep on keeping on?

Be committed and intrinsically motivated. Write your vision and start with the end in mind. What does the big picture look like? Write the vision, copy and paste the vision, record the vision, do whatever legally, morally, and ethically that you need to do so the provision can show up. What one person can do, anyone can do if the desire and passion is there. I believe in you and in the beauty of your dreams. When you get sick and tired of being sick and tired, you will act. I trust that when you do, you will join me, Lucinda Cross…. together we will create a business beyond your wildest dreams!

DESIGNING YOUR LIFESTYLE BY CRAFTING YOUR VISION BOARD

Where visions are limited, the only thing I could rely on was my vision board. A piece of cut out paper from magazines and affirmations, pictures of freedom and wealth is all I had when it came to creative visualization for my vision board, which was actually a vision journal then. I decided to create what I would like to see myself doing in the future by cutting out inspirational quotes and images that I could look at daily to give me hope and inspiration.

When is the last time you put your vision on paper. I am not talking about a thirty-page business plan or the hottest self-improvement seminar that you went to, and had to fill out a questionnaire or assessment. I am talking elementary school taking glue, pictures, colors, and phrases and placing your vision on a board. This concept known as a Vision Board is a visual explorer.

It is our thinking, more than our surroundings, which determines our level of happiness. Hold a thought and you will create an emotion. That emotion drives a behavior, which in turn creates an event. To change your events you must first change your vision.

The challenge, for most of us, is to move from pessimistic thinking to where your thoughts create feelings of hope and joy. So how do you do it? Simple, no secret, you create a Vision Board or better yet do what I do, have a Vision Board Party where you get a group of friends together with magazines, books, anything visual, and you cut out pictures that represent how you envision your life/business in the future.

This whole process helps you turn your visions into reality and watch your goals come to fruition right before your EYES.

The concept of vision boards has been around for years; I actually started researching this concept several years ago. When I was in prison, I had no idea they called it a vision board, I called it "The future". To date, I have accomplished 80% of my goals for my life and business that I place on my vision board including my husband. Most people have a difficult time creating a life plan or business plan and a difficult time believing in the success of accomplishing their goals, but this visual process will give you the motivation you need to go after "What's been holding you back". I now go from state to state conducting vision board parties for groups and organizations, it is quite fun to see others create their vision board as I am living and fulfilling mine at the same time.

Here are some tools you will need to create your vision board:

- Create a vision board that includes pictures of things that you would like to have in life. Include things that you know you cannot afford right now, but if money were not an option you would have it right now. Items could include a vacation, a new house, a husband, wife, children and of course more money and health. The pictures can come from anywhere such as magazines, computer printouts, and newspapers.
- Place the vision board where you will see it throughout the day.
- Look at each picture on your vision board at least daily, and daydream about having that thing now. Allow yourself to be fully engaged in the daydream, and have fun with it.

Enjoy your visual creation and please keep your eye on the prize.

Chapter 11:
Do not Worry About the HOW

On the *Road to Redemption*, the bigger vision is what will keep you motivated. Worrying about how you will get to your destination or how you will get things done will hold you back. Worrying about the "How" is not as important as the "What". Let me explain; if you are still in your little box, with big ideas, looking for the big payday, it may be time to create a bigger box for your vision. Staying in the box is not the problem, when we begin to think out the box and have not used all our resources in the box that is when we miss the big Pay Day. Your Pay Day can be in the form of money, resources, new job, promotion, new relationship, and so on.

Making a transition from being told what to do and not do in prison, then to come home and be told what to do and not do in a halfway house, then to get in a relationship to be told what to do and not do at work -- I was tired of being bullied by society. I wanted to get my power and authority back. I wanted to use my gifts without restraints and bars, without limits and boundaries.

Look at your gift and figure out how you can reach a larger audience, reach a ready-made opportunity to which you can present and contribute your best skills and gifts. We have these wealthy assets, these abundant gifts and talents, we know how to use them, we have used them before, we know they work, we know we are blessed, we know how serious our gifts are and we have seen the results they produce in others' lives. Here is the important question. How can we use our gifts to live an abundant lifestyle, start a ministry, start a business, open my restaurant, write a book, or speak to the public...?

Well I am going to ask you to let go of the how today. You should not be worrying about the how. Your focus should be aligning yourself and connecting your gifts to your purpose to receive the resources.

When you concentrate, on the How you restrict your abilities. You place limits and boundaries on what can and cannot happen by thinking about "How" this can get done or "How it will get done. Let God do his business. You make the necessary connections, call the person in charge, send in your information, and walk into that bank, doing your research, networking with the right people, affiliating yourself with those already doing it.

The HOW will take care of itself. The WHAT is your job, what can you do to perfect your skill, what can you do to operate at your highest and best, what can you do differently today, what can you do to be prepared, what is on your agenda this week that moves you closer to your vision, what numbers should you call, what are you doing in the morning to get closer to your God for clarity?

Are you asking the right questions? Are you commanding your mornings? What are you doing in the evening to make sure your mind is right for the HOW answer to show up in your most vulnerable state of rest?

Write the one thing that you can create to expose yourself (talents, skills, and gifts).

For example: can you create a motivational audio CD, an e-book that people can download, an event, a product, a journal, a T-shirt, a workbook the list goes on.

Here is the key; you must give yourself permission to succeed. After you give yourself permission to succeed, you have to grant yourself the gift of laser sharp focus.

Permission to succeed means that you give yourself permission to take risks, permission to speak your mind, permission to say no to others and yes to yourself.

You can choose who you want to become and what you want to do without breaking any moral or governmental laws. To be successful you must first step back and realize that you have to give yourself permission.

Marianne Williamson said it so eloquently in her book, *A Return to Love*,

> There is nothing enlightening about shrinking so others will not feel insecure around you...your playing small does not serve the world...as we let our own light shine, we unconsciously give others permission to do the same. As we are liberated from our own fear, our presence automatically liberates others.

When we believe in ourselves and set an intention, key word here is Intention to do something, we become an attractor, a magnet and draw to ourselves the people and resources we need. We accept the invitation to abundance according to the book of Isaiah.

Will it be easy?
Is it easy?
Unlikely, nothing worthwhile is easy.

Will it be rewarding?
Will it be fulfilling?
Absolutely.

To succeed in life and on the *Road to Redemption* you must first give yourself permission to succeed. Despite your current state, this means you have to develop a positive inner dialogue. Are your thoughts supporting you or limiting you?

You cannot change what you do not acknowledge. Get real with yourself about your life and everybody in it. Be truthful about what is not working in your life. Stop making excuses and start making results.

The beauty of redemption, reinvention, and recovering is the fact that we all have a story to tell, we are all gifted with creative self-expression, and we are unique in our own right. Authenticity has no competition so my story is just as powerful as your story.

Promise yourself that you will no longer be a victim of the past, self-sabotage, guilt, unworthiness, and so on...

I could not imagine what my life would be as if I did not remove my self-limiting thoughts, behavior and habits. I stepped out of prison into boot camp into the halfway house and into society feeling well deserving of a better life.

- What if you deserved then and deserve now, so much more and so much better?
- What if you were wrong and it is not your fault?
- What if your mother was too weak or your father was too weak to protect you, to believe you, to understand you?
- What if it is you, not "them" who has been keeping you in that mental prison all of this time?
- What if I told you right here, right now, all you had to do is _____ to be free, to be successful, to activate. Would you do it? Would you believe in you to do it?

Tell me are you sick and tired of being sick and tired to the point you will stand for yourself right now and declare your right to a better life, whoever you have to face, whatever you have to do? Will you grab on? Will you stand straight? Will you look fear in the eye?

I want you to evaluate if you are a:

Skunk: Always with a chip on your shoulder, easily offended and always finding something that is not right with yourself and others.

Bear: trying to control everyone and everything. Dominating or intimidating everyone with whom you interact. The type that tells others what they are thinking and feeling.

Mouse: Everything is just extra for you, comments are extra, and a person looking at you is extra. You over analyze just about everything and you often ASSume wrong. This is also known as the drama queen.

Cat: everything is done to you, you are the captive, and you whine most of the time and complain. You often blame others and expect everyone to treat you in a specific way.

Let us get one thing clear, you are an overcomer, overachiever, victorious, unstoppable and unshakable. This is what you need for laser sharp focus.

Having laser sharp focus is crucial to your long-term success. Having a good idea and sticking with it until it either succeeds or fails is actually a crucial skill – A skill that many entrepreneurs unfortunately lack and fail as a result. Many entrepreneurs suffer from a severe disease called the "Shiny Object Syndrome"

Results Come with Persistence, not Singular Spurts of Effort.

People often feel powerful spurts of desire, of determination, of feeling as if they are willing to do whatever it takes. Feeling that way for a few days or weeks is common. However, to succeed you really need to be able to stay motivated and inspired about what you are doing for months and years at a time.

Your Focus Must Be Laser Sharp:

Life lessons is not a short-term game, business is not a fly-by-night success. You have wins and you have losses. It is a matter of persisting through all the difficulties to the result of real success. That takes time and focus.

Improve Your Focus with Productivity Systems
Your habits play a large role in how focused you stay.

One habit that many successful business people have is planning their day at the beginning of the day. When you wake up, the first thing you do is get out a sheet of paper and write exactly what you want to accomplish today. Then, write what you want to accomplish this week, then this month, then this year, then your three-year goals.

If you have inspiring goals set, this will help you stay focused on both the short-term actions and the long-term picture. Doing this every day will help you stay motivated in doing what you need to do to succeed. You will have a clear picture of what the success of completing the goals look like and you will work harder to get them complete as opposed to going after every "to-do" on your list.

Finally, on the *Road to Redemption* you have to be activated. This state of mind means that you will not forget how important it is to have a relationship with you and God. You must be in alignment with your destiny. You must prepare and equip yourself for the journey. This means that you will demand nothing less than the best for yourself and of yourself. There is neither anything wrong with wanting to live life as if it is golden, nor with demanding dignity, love, honor, peace, and harmonious relationships in your life.

Take a stand right now that you are worthy of living life on purpose despite your past mistakes. You must believe that you deserve the best and you are not selfish, naive, ignorant, or delusional to expect it. It is not a motivational power puff presentation to believe that God has provision for your vision, resources for your needs and a person destined to be with you for the rest of your life happily. Here is the secret; you have to believe that you are worth the investment that God has given you. You have to believe that you are worth the healing that loves brings, when you are not used to being loved. For this *Road to Redemption* to be activated, you must consciously decide to actively, purposefully work on improving your life each day.

You do not have to live institutionalized; recidivism can be reduced, by removing yourself from the mental prison we have placed ourselves in. You can be free by using the keys that God has given you freely.

This *Road to Redemption* is not a want or an intention that you make, this is not even a declaration or decree that you work on. This is something you do every day; discipline yourself to do the work, to make the transition. If you can wash, eat and sleep everyday without someone telling you to do it, the same goes for Activation. You must learn how to self-motivate when there is no conference call, tele-seminar or workshop. You must learn to act when everything and anything that could go wrong, does go wrong.

We all deserve to have loving, harmonious relationships, lavish wealth, ideal health. Gift yourself permission to be you, to be authentically you.

Chapter 12:
The Butterfly Emerges

As I walk out the gates of FPC Federal Prison Camp in Bryan Texas, I fly toward hope. My wings are full of Redemption.

As I walk out on the cafeteria floor in Mercy College as they call my name, I fly toward success. My wings are full of Resilience.

As I am carried into the nursery to see the face of my firstborn in Our Lady of Mercy Hospital, I fly toward love. My wings are full of Responsibility.

As I hand in my letter of resignation from my job to pursue my entrepreneurial journey, I fly toward opportunity. My wings are full of Reinvention.

As I received my first interview on ABC News for my first book "Corporate Mom Drop Outs", I fly toward commitment. My wings are full of Clarity.

As I walk down the aisle to become a wife in Greater Anointing Tabernacle, I fly toward love. My wings are full of joy.

As I write this book, I fly toward truth. My wings are full of Freedom. Free after being in the cocoon, allowing the inner man to purge itself to become something greater.

I want to stress that these are learned skills, and this is acquired knowledge in this book. Use this book and its information as a way to raising your children to never give up, competing in the workplace, and not allowing someone's position to intimidate you, understand you are more than a job description so show up powerfully every day, selling yourself or your products, and adding true value, or gaining confidence, trust and affection from those you respect, love and value.

The hardest part in learning something new is unlearning the old way of doing it. I had to learn that not everybody could download information in my motherboard "mind". We have to be careful from whom and from where we get our information, because there are people with degrees, certificates and the whole nine yards, but they cannot chew gum and walk. Then there are the wise ones who have nothing fancy to brag about but are full of wisdom, knowledge, and understanding. You want to add to what is already inside you, you do not need seek outside sources of what is inside, and you just need to add to what you have.

The teachers that I have encountered in those five years imparted so much information that I had no choice but to push forward when I thought about giving up inside the prison and outside. You never know who has the answers to your questions.

I had to learn that the person I spend the most time with is myself. The person I need to influence the most is myself. The person whose characteristics and behavior patterns that need eliminating or improving is mine. I had to hold myself accountable. If you do not hold yourself accountable, you will misdiagnose every problem you have. You will mistreat the biggest and most infected issues.

I had to ask myself the following:

- What did I do to make this result happen?
- Did I trust foolishly and was I being naïve?

- Did I ignore any of the warning signs?
- Did I fail to be clear about what I expected?
- Did I choose the wrong people or place?
- Did I fail to stand for myself and speak my truth?
- Did I act out of ill motives?
- Did I fail to tell someone to leave me alone?
- Did I fail to say not this time, this time is for me?
- Did I fail to be truthful with others and myself? Why?
- Did I forgive myself first?
- Did I give myself permission to love, live or learn openly?

Answering these questions will help you as it helped me look in the one right place instead of a thousand wrong places for solutions to your problems and answers to your questions.

Throughout all I have been through when I was locked down, I was not locked out. Locked down physically but not locked out of life, my life. It was no longer about what others were doing to me, why was I set up? Why did they snitch on me? Why did I say yes? Moreover, I started saying, what can I do to turn around this situation? Once I figured out the formula for HOPE, I could program myself for success.

I had to forgive myself, hold myself responsible, and not blame anyone else for where I was in prison and later in life.

Becoming a convict was not a label I accepted, a single mom is not a label I accepted, being broke and poor was not a label I accepted. I accepted responsibility.

No one but you is going to get you out of the mess you are in or was in. You can stop going to tarot card readers, rock throwers, frog kissers, looking for that magic ball and start working with

- IN you.
- IN the choices you made
- IN the words you said
- IN the anger you dispersed
- IN settling for less
- IN marrying him or her
- IN inviting him or her in
- IN the feelings you have
- IN the falseness you showed
- IN quitting
- IN deciding you are not worth it
- IN taking one more hit
- IN leaving that job and not having a plan
- IN eating that unhealthy meal plus snacks
- IN letting them talk you into it
- IN believing them/him/her
- IN accepting that treatment
- IN letting them/him/her come back
- IN not forgiving yourself or other

I had to strip away from any of the excuses I might have had about who I was, where I was, and why I was where I was in life. This was bigger than twenty-three-hour lockdown, bigger than the prison doors; this was bigger than the emotional and mental abuse I allowed others to exercise on me. I had to go "IN", to get "OUT" with a free spirit. Free from any weights that might have held me down from flying, as I was created to do.

Accept the premise that the only time is now. Right now. The past is over and your future has not happened yet, but you can sit around waiting for something to happen or you can make something worthwhile happen. Dreams, plans, and opportunities are just waiting for you to pick them up.

Consider this your wake-up call. I am just making you aware of the greatness inside you. If God can use me to uplift, empower, and inspire others, so can you. Use this awareness to create a different experience in life. Be a willing spirit, lean forward and let go.

Keep in mind the transformation process happened for me when it was just me with no children, no husband, no business ideas, no church home, and no coach. It was God and I. I had to stand on my own two feet, fight my way out, and declare that I would no longer be a victim.

I had to create my own experience; I had to reclaim my life. I had to declare my right to a better life, regardless of whom I had to face and what I had to do. I am grabbing on, I am committed to leaving a legacy for my children. How about you? What are you committed to do? Will you grab on even if it means to take two steps back to take ten steps forward?

Getting real with yourself about life and everybody in it is important. Being truthful about what is working and what is not working in life is crucial in the cocooning process. Stop making excuses, stop complaining, and start making real results that accelerate you forward.

My comeback is a result of my mindset shifting. Linking my vision + my passion = my mission. You were born to be outstanding and the world has a need "of" you. In fact, the world has been preparing you to fill this need with one life experience after another.

Finding and fulfilling your potential will lead your highest experience in life. Believe you have a mission. Your mission is your calling, your lifework. It is not a job, a role or a goal that we can just check off from our "to-do" list.

Your mission is greater. Do you see yourself as someone who can make a difference? If you answered yes then I suggest you find your vision and watch how your life changes. If you see yourself as someone who can make a difference this must be a decision made from the heart. This is not a thought, this is a conviction that you live by all of the time, not when you have time, when you feel like it, or when you are bored, this is a matter of principle. This is a demand you are placing on yourself, accepting the fact that you will no longer live in your comfort zone; you are not going to avoid achieving or accomplishing positive momentum.

Manage your life with purpose you are the manager of your emotional, social, spiritual, and physical life. Manage it with purpose, manage it with knowledge, and manage it with understanding and wisdom.

- You have made it this far.
- I have made it this far
- It is your turn now
- You are smart enough
- You are good enough
- You are a winner
- You are accepted
- You are a woman with a powerful voice
- You are the right age
- You have the right weight
- You are more than enough
- You do believe
- You do trust
- You know what to say
- You know how to act

- You know where you are going
- You know when to go
- You know when to stay
- You are worth it
- You are the most beautiful butterfly the world has ever seen.

Believe you have a mission, wherever you are, whatever you have been through, the world has a need "of" you at your highest and best.

Your vision is going to inspire you, as my vision did for me in 2006 when I handed in my letter of resignation. Your vision is going to renew your creative fire. Your vision will mobilize people and resources to align with your vision.

In your transition, you must be willing to reposition yourself. 80% of this shift will happen in you first.

As a mom of three wonderful children, a wife to a man that I believe is a true angel, a daughter to a mother who raised me the best she could and did a good job at it, with what she had, a daughter to a father who always called me a princess and the greatest gift he has ever had.

I am now free and flying. God directs my life. I travel across the states to speak, empower, and uplift women to become leaders in their community.

I have overcome overwhelming personal difficulties to become the author, speaker, coach, talk show host, and woman of God. My walk in the dark valley was an experience that made me into the powerful vessel I am today. I have emerged at a far different place and space from where I started at in my twenties and with a far more positive perspective on life. I am able to use my creative self-expression to host workshops and seminars in different states.

I use my speaking and writing abilities to educate women of all colors, nationalities, and ages, to create a better life for themselves and their communities, by discovering that God did not give up on them, and they should not give up on God.

I started a movement with Corporate Mom Drop Outs, woman who believed in themselves and their families, I am the founder of Praying Moms, which is an organization that proclaims to be the new P. T. A. in town, we pray and act to give mothers nationwide hope. We conducted our first annual Prayer Walk in Central Park, which spanned out to five other states in 2011.

As a flying butterfly, I have experienced a journey of redemption and healing from despair to hope and self-reliance. From my colorful background or rap sheet, I have emerged as a winner, achieving success on my own terms, committed to an eclectic message of power and determination. I push myself to be a speaker with a message and a prolific author; I can now take my audience and readers by the hand and lead them down the path of discovery, empowerment, love, and support, based on my own life's experiences and observations.

I went from thinking of me being a convict to being a child of God, from a troubled young girl to a daughter of the most high. This means that I am unique, ordinary and dedicated to doing unique and extraordinary things.

I believe that every woman has gifts, talents, dreams, and goals that she desires to accomplish in her lifetime and to be appreciated, encouraged and understood.

My mission is to provide programs and products, which greatly enhance our lives; enable us to have fruitful, satisfying lives; increase in our personal and professional success; and to connect us to other women where we can be each other's cheerleader through this transitional life process. My intention is to **uplift, empower, inspire, support, and encourage** each other to be free to transform into all that we are intended to be.

My programs and services promote uplifting, positive relationships to meet you where you are. I would not be able to stand if I did not grow through, what I had to go through.

Do you believe that YOU are endowed with the same seeds of greatness as anyone you have ever envied or admired? You have value, passion and you do not have to settle for less than the attainment of your dreams.

Recognize your value, discover your passion, and run in hot pursuit toward it. You can excel. You do have significance. You can unearth the life you deserve and for which you were destined!

I thank you for reading this book and I pray it was what you needed to support you in activating your power. As the founder of ***Activate! Dynamic Transitions and Powerful Transformations***, my purpose is to influence your life through a series of inspirational messages geared toward improving your communication, inner image, relationships, and entrepreneurial/career endeavors. My hope and dream is that you will allow me to come alongside you, to empower you gradually to become more confident, successful, and positive.

Every woman deserves to achieve her own striking change in appearance, character, or circumstances that brings her the culmination of dreams and ambitions (whether they are secret or shared with others). What a powerful opportunity we have to exemplify the beauty, strength, grace, fortitude, and exciting new adventures that await every woman who says, **Yes, I CAN** move onward and upward no matter what has transpired in my life!

Women get excited to hear that mother's prayers are answered, that trials do pass, that a painful past can be left behind, and a transition and transformation can take place. Strength and beauty come as the roots of faith are nurtured, and become food for our souls and minds.

We can:

- acquire greater self-respect, draw healthy boundaries, create an impressive new look,
- take classes for personal and professional growth, learn to laugh at ourselves,
- and extend a victorious smile everyday of our lives!

Let us sing the song in our hearts, let us dance to the beat of our own tune. We have overcome, and we can rise to new heights of personal and professional success despite our past.

Together, we can choose to live life to the fullest so get ready! I will be continuing the process of my own **personal transition and transformation** right with you!

Let us fly together.

Lucinda Cross

Please visit www.lucindacross.com to hire Lucinda Cross for speaking engagements. To sign up for her programs please visit www.lucindacross.com

To e-mail Lucinda Cross your thoughts and testimonial please e-mail her assistant at assistant@lucindacross.com

"Free at last, Free at last, I thank God almighty I am free at last." (Dr. Martin Luther King)

Mark 3:3 Jesus said to the man who had the withered hand, "Step forward."

So therefore, Step forward on your Road to Redemption...